FEAST OR FAMINE?

FEAST OR FAMINE?

How the Gospel challenges austerity

**An Ekklesia Lent course
for groups and individuals**

EDITED BY SIMON BARROW

with PAT BENNETT, JOHN GILLIBRAND,
KEITH HEBDEN, SAVITRI HENSMAN,
BERNADETTE MEADEN,
VIRGINIA MOFFATT and JILL SEGGER

DARTON · LONGMAN + TODD

First published in 2017 by
Darton, Longman and Todd Ltd
1 Spencer Court
140-142 Wandsworth High Street
London SW18 4JJ

ISBN: 978-0-232-53261-6

A catalogue record for this book is available from the British Library.

Designed and produced by Judy Linard

Printed and bound in Great Britain by Bell & Bain, Glasgow

CONTENTS

FEAST OR FAMINE?

FOREWORD

This five-week Lent course for groups and individuals looks at the practical issues of economic austerity versus plenty in modern Britain and across the world. It is based on the core gospel theme of feast versus famine. Its central message is that in the way of Christ we can learn to grow together through sharing; whereas we are divided by hoarding and by the grotesque inequality that lies at the heart of our current global economic arrangements.

St Augustine once observed that, 'charity is no substitute for justice withheld.' In other words, individual acts of generosity, no matter how well intentioned, cannot dispense with the need to stand alongside the victims of an inequitable and unfair ordering of society, or the quest to see that right is done. (This is also recognised in another DLT Lent resource which can be used alongside *Feast or Famine*; the book, by Virginia Moffatt, is called *Nothing More and Nothing Less* and is based on the film *I, Daniel Blake*.)

To acknowledge this is to recognise plainly that closing the gap between the poor and the rich, alongside pursuing justice for 'the widow and orphan' (archetypes of the socially excluded in biblical times), are major biblical themes. Indeed, as US evangelical leader Jim Wallis has pointed out, the Bible has more to say about wealth and poverty – condemning both as signs of a social order straying from the will of God – than any other single topic.

Renewing our understanding of what all this means for individuals, churches and communities is vital. It can transform the way we respond to the ideology, practice and impact of austerity on the most vulnerable in society, both locally and globally. It also enables us to understand the Gospel is *both* personal *and* social in its implications for the way we live, and the belief that sustains a new and different way of living.

It is in this context that this book and course sets out (in straightforward, non-technical terms) what the ideology of austerity is, what impact it has had, why it offers no solution to the deep wounds afflicting our society, and how the sociality of the church can help create an alternative way of thinking and acting based on generosity, hospitality and filial solidarity.

These themes are especially appropriate for Lent, when Christians remember Christ's period of fasting in the desert – a time of radical reorientation. This was the period in his ministry when he resisted the blandishments of an unjust ruler, committed to his mission of deliverance for all who are oppressed, and invited his followers to renew themselves spiritually in responding to the Good News of human and divine reconciliation in all areas of life.

Simon Barrow
November 2017

ACKNOWLEDGEMENTS

The editor and contributors would like to thank all who have made this book and course possible. In particular, our publisher, David Moloney, for his forbearance when the project was subject to difficult delay, and to all at DLT for their professionalism. Also to Ekklesia's current contract staff and board members: Jill Segger, Bob Carling, Luke Dowding, Kate Guthrie and Vaughan Jones. They do an incredible amount with very little, and in that sense (and many others) are active anti-austerity agents! Particular appreciation goes to Pat Bennett and the Iona Community for the prayer material and resources. Additional thanks to Dr Simon Duffy and the marvellous Centre for Welfare Reform, with whom we often cooperate on these important issues – and to Carla J. Roth, as ever. Also to Jenny D'Esterre, Ann Pettifor, Richard Murphy and Frances Coppola (even though they may not always agree with each other, or what we say here!) for stimulation and inspiration. This book is dedicated to the late Catherine Harkin and to Carrie Gooch (who have both shown such exemplary and un-austere generosity) and to the memory of Mennonite theologian Alan Kreider, who sadly passed away as it was being completed.

INTRODUCTION

Moving Beyond Austerity:
A Christian Challenge

SIMON BARROW

*The master replied, 'You wicked, lazy servant! So
you knew that I harvest where I have not sown
and gather where I have not scattered seed? Well
then, you should have put my money on deposit
with the bankers, so that when I returned I would
have received it back with interest.*

*'So take the bag of gold from him and give it
to the one who has ten bags. For whoever has will
be given more, and they will have an abundance.
Whoever does not have, even what they have will
be taken from them.'*

(Matthew 25:26-29)

'Austerity' is a word that has been regularly bandied
about in the news media for over a decade now, most
particularly since the global economic crash of 2007/8.
In 2017 there was some talk after the General Election of
it abating. But in reality it is likely to be with us for some
years to come, particularly as we grapple with Brexit and
with other structural problems in the global economy.

So what does austerity really mean? What is its
impact on our thinking and behaviour? Above all, why

should it be a concern for Christians and the focus of a book with a Lent theme?

If you stop someone in the street and ask them what 'austerity' is, you are likely to get an answer along the lines that it is to do with a shortage of money, meaning that we all have to tighten our belts. The words 'debt', 'deficit' and 'cutbacks' will most likely be thrown in there, too.

That's definitely along the right initial lines, both in terms of identifying the belt-tightening rhetoric of most government spending discussions today, and in a slight vagueness about what it all amounts to.

Politicians, especially those speaking on behalf of governments, are liable to throw other phrases into the interpretative mix: namely, 'difficult decisions have to be made' and 'we're all in this together'.

There will often be a tinge of regret present, too. 'It's a shame we have to make cuts', someone will say. 'It's hard on people. But unfortunately there's no real alternative. We just have to face up to reality.'

Come to think of it, this all does begin to sound rather penitential, doesn't it? We've been 'living beyond our means', but now we have to shape up and start to prune back. 'It will be painful, but in the long run it's necessary, unavoidable and beneficial to our health as individuals and a nation', as one parliamentarian put it to me not so long ago.

Indeed, such language finds strong echoes in many popular presentations about Lent, with the typical emphasis on 'giving things up', slimming down and getting fit again. 'No gain without a bit of pain', as the fitness video mantra has it. (Along with the fad for new diets, that's as near as many get to the old tradition of fasting these days!)

Other apparent echoes of the Bible are also there.

INTRODUCTION

Feast or Famine? is a not insignificant theme in the part of the biblical text that Christians call the Old Testament, but which also constitutes the Hebrew Scriptures – a shared narrative about divine deliverance. In the ancient world, this inevitably had strong overtones of bare survival in the face of a cycle of good times and bad times. Think of the story of Joseph's prophecy in the book of Genesis 41:29-30:

> *Behold, seven years of great abundance are coming in all the land of Egypt; and after them seven years of famine will come, and all the abundance will be forgotten in the land of Egypt, and the famine will ravage the land. So the abundance will be unknown in the land because of that subsequent famine; for it will be very severe.*

What I want to do in this introductory chapter to our five-fold course (Spending or Saving? Hunger or Satisfaction? Health or Wealth? Security or Insecurity? and Cutting or Investing?) is to look at what is at stake in this business of austerity, in the season of Lent, and in the question of facing the feast/famine contrast between want and plenty.

In the first instance this requires tackling some pretty major misunderstandings which have crept into our language and thinking, and which this book is in large part seeking to combat – or at least to point us away from, and towards a different, more hopeful conversation.

Austerity: a choice, not a necessity

Let's start again with austerity. In general parlance it means 'sternness or severity of manner or attitude'. It comes from the French *austérité* via the Latin *austeritas*, from *austerus*, or 'severe'. Economists use the term to denote the decision to cut public spending (that is, local or national government expenditure) in order to reduce the annual deficit between government earnings and outgoings, and/or the overall debt the country has (what is owed to others). That 'and/or' should be noted, because 'deficit' and 'debt' are wrongly used interchangeably, but are different things. We will come back to that shortly.

The important thing to note here is that, although bodies like the International Monetary Fund and the European Central Bank have often been known, through collective political sanction, effectively to *impose* 'austerity policies' on governments (the catastrophic case of Greece in recent years comes immediately to mind), at every level what we call austerity is a *choice*. It is about not using resources one way, in order to use them another way.

This choice is often disguised by language about apparent necessity. 'We are closing public libraries, cutting welfare payments, reducing the care budget, axing women's aid centres and imposing benefit sanctions not because we want to – but because we have to *for economic reasons*.' That is the clear message. It is a false one. In fact the best, simple definition of austerity (and one of the first definitions you will find if you use a popular Internet search engine) is, 'difficult economic conditions created by government measures to reduce public expenditure.'

That's right. The conditions are created by the decision. And the decision is to cut public spending (not the much larger mounting pile of financial or household debt, note), with all the consequences that has for people and communities, as well as for the economic and social health of society as a whole.

INTRODUCTION

But back to necessity. If cutting public spending is harmful (and looking at the state of public services impacting some of the poorest and most vulnerable in society leaves you with the clear message that it is), why do so many politicians and parties want to do it? The answer that they tend to give is that 'we have to', otherwise the deficit will rise inexorably, and we will drown in debt.

Let's look at those claims. First, Britain, along with many other countries, does have a mountain of debt. That's true. At the time of writing it is some £1.8 trillion pounds. An absolutely eye-watering sum. But globally it is far from the largest. The biggest debtor in the world is not a so-called third world or developing country, but the United States, which owes about $18.96 trillion.

Debt is, in fact, what makes the world go round financially. Some 70 to 80 per cent of the global economy is not based on making and selling things but on financial services and speculation. (That is a massive imbalance which had a lot to do with the 2008 collapse, incidentally). Debt is a fatal problem when creditors make demands on you and you cannot pay (like Greece). For the wealthy, however, debt can be and often is a constantly deferred credit line and quite a nice advantage. By contrast, if you are poor, debt (or rather, the way it is handled by the rich) can kill you. That happens in impoverished parts of the world every day.

In the case of Britain's debt, the annual cost of servicing it (interest payments) is around £44 billion (which is roughly 3 per cent of GDP or 8 per cent of UK government tax income). That's large, but not life threatening. In fact – and this is really important – the largest proportion of our national debt is, as we've already mentioned in passing, that accumulating in households and financial institutions. 'Austerity' (cutting public expenditure) does nothing to reduce that. Indeed it mostly increases it, because when people face cutbacks they borrow more.

Cutting public expenditure doesn't really reduce debt; it simply transfers it from one place to another. The only thing that genuinely reduces debt is producing and selling enough to pay it off, and if the economy is rocky and investment is falling or wobbling (as it has been in recent years), then that won't happen.

Indeed many economists (like those associated with the New Economics Foundation and other friends of Ekklesia) argue persuasively that we actually need to *increase* public spending in order to reduce debt – making sure that money is spent on the right things to get the economy moving, to reduce the burden on households, and to get out of a spiral of low wages and low taxes (which reduces government income and makes life harder for everybody). One such non-partisan plan has been called 'the Green New Deal' (http://www.greennewdealgroup.org). It is about facing the triple burden of the global credit crunch / lack of demand, 'peak oil' (the time when the maximum rate of extraction of petroleum is reached) and the urgent need to address climate change and global warming. What it proposes, in simple terms, is a huge increase in public investment in green technology, construction and services that would produce a boom in jobs and economic activity. Pretty much the opposite of austerity, therefore.

This makes a good deal of sense. Certainly more sense than bailing out private banks while not fundamentally reforming the financial sector, pouring money into unfocused 'quantitative easing' (the introduction of new money into the money supply by a central bank), spending over £205 billion on renewing the unnecessary and immoral Trident nuclear weapons programme, or watching poorer families and communities crushed by lack of resources for essential services.

Why don't we do this, then? Partly because those who actually benefit from austerity (including corporate tax avoiders and recipients of some £60 billion worth of tax cuts at a time when spending on social security and social care is being slashed) don't want it. To repeat, austerity is a choice. And in recent years the choice has been to take money from those who have least of it, and give it to those who have most. As it says in Matthew 25 (and not in an approving way, as I shall show), 'For whoever has will be given more, and they will have an abundance. Whoever does not have, even what they have will be taken from them.'

The reason for this choice, politicians often say, is that putting money in the hands of the wealthy and big corporations through cutting tax enables them to invest, which in turn gets the economy moving. However, the evidence for this is scarce. Mostly, this money gets spent or squirreled away as a kind of windfall. There is no necessary relation between a tax reduction and productive investment. In many cases (as in the high profile ones involving some of our largest global corporations), little if any 'domestic' tax is paid at all. This requires further urgent action.

The other big justification for austerity cuts, the actual impact of which we explore throughout this course, are that they redress the imbalance between the state and other economic actors (with the implication that government is 'too big') and that it is necessary to tackle the deficit and debt.

In relation to the size and role of government, that is

a huge debate. Ekklesia has argued over the years that a 'courageous state' (to adopt the title of an important book by Richard Murphy) is needed to support investment in public good. That doesn't mean the government can or should do everything. Far from it. What it does mean is that money aggregated and dispersed throughout the whole of society can and must, as in the case of the NHS at its best, ensure that resources are spread and used fairly and justly. Alongside that we need something like a 'Green New Deal' (supported by civic groups and people from several political parties and none) referred to above, and partnerships with private and voluntary initiative which are not about replacing statutory provision with insecure charity, but are about building a genuine common good in which we really are 'all in it together' (whereas the current reality of growing inequality in the UK shows that we are not).

The deficit obsession: why austerity fails and makes us suffer

Meanwhile, the deficit issue is critical. It has almost become an obsession in recent years, with the mainstream media following politicians in regarding the reduction of shortfalls in the annual national income-expenditure balance sheet as an economic sacred cow – despite the fact that governments have consistently missed targets to achieve this over the past decade. In fact, if we are to reduce overall debt by expanding economic activity in appropriate and beneficial ways (generalised 'growth' without attention to whether what is growing is good, like green energy, or bad, like burning fossil fuels, is an unhelpful moniker), then for a time, at least, the annual account deficit may need to increase in order to allow resources to flow into the right places. Like homes to address the housing need (especially following the horrific Grenfell Tower fire), health and social care to keep us fit and active, and productive work to support the economy.

Some months ago, the Chancellor of the Exchequer said that he was expecting government borrowing to fall in 2017. His new fiscal rules (those concerning government revenue collection and spending) would provide 'headroom' for more borrowing than currently forecast, he declared. After her narrow election victory in June 2017 the Prime Minister also talked about attenuating austerity in this way. The notion of 'headroom' illustrates a basic fallacy, however. The national economy is effectively being compared to a household budget (the false analogy Margaret Thatcher popularised), on the basis that we can thereby only responsibly spend what we have already brought in.

But in fact the government and the banks can do something you and I cannot do. They can create credit (which is what money actually is) and can use that to generate activity that then enlarges our income and begins to pay down debt – reducing its cost and its drag effect. This is a game changer. So in the short run, government spending may quite properly need to increase in order to produce the longer-term effect we want. Cutting the deficit is not an automatic route to cutting debt, and may actually make the situation worse. As PRIME Economics put it to the *Financial Times* in January 2017:

> *The health or otherwise of the public finances depends entirely on the health of the economy. By focusing excessively on fiscal policy, and not on the creation of skilled, well-paid, tax-generating employment, policy-makers have repeatedly missed*

fiscal targets. Their approach can be compared to looking through the wrong end of a telescope.

In short, as an economic mechanism there is little evidence that austerity actually works (because it starves us of resources at the time we need them most) and it certainly contributes hugely to public misery – the principle issue addressed in this course.

The need to change our belief system

So why do these issues continue to be so widely misunderstood by the public, most of whom seem to believe that austerity is a necessity not a choice, and most of whom, when polled, think that 'fiscal tightening' (cuts) will do the job of getting things back on track? Fundamentally, it is to do with two things, deeply rooted in our belief system.

The first is the belief that money is a commodity that can be in short supply. That's true for you and me, but it isn't true of the national or global economy. Because while some 'money' – a very small percentage – is cash, most of it is notional ('fiat currency', as it's known). That is, a vast network of expanding, ultimately unquantifiable contracts which depend on book keeping entries but are not backed up by notes, gold, or anything else we might imagine exists to make money 'real'. As political economist Ann Pettifor explained in an interview in *Vogue* magazine (http://www.vogue.com/article/money-and-the-government-how-it-works-ann-pettifor) about her vital book, *The Production of Money: How to Break the Power of Bankers* (Verso, 2017):

As the economist Joseph Schumpeter has said, money is nothing more than a promise, a promise to pay. It's a social construct. Coins, checks, the credit card you hand over at the till –t hey're representative of those promises. We're trained to think of money as a commodity, something there's a limited supply of, that you can either spend or save, but in fact we're creating money all the time, by making these promises. When you use a credit card, you're not handing over your card to the shopkeeper or the waiter to keep, you're just showing them a piece of plastic that says, 'this person can be trusted'. We make myriad uses of these arrangements every day. And there's far more of those promises in circulation at any given time than there is hard money sitting in vaults, or in people's wallets, or wherever.

What that means is that while you and I may be wise not to spend too much unless we have the right amount of cash or credit, governments and banks can generate the power for things to happen by issuing credit, and need to do so especially when things are tough and need turning around. (Doing this too much or randomly can produce too much inflation and other problems, but that's another matter.) Money, in other words, is a means of negotiating relationships, choices and transactions – and how we create, use and spend it tells us a lot about who we are and what we want. At the moment it seems to be telling us that we want to live in a grossly unequal world, to base our lives on carbon energy that is destroying the planet, and to allow the poorest and those least able to survive without support (actually *none* of us can survive without support) to go to the wall.

This can and must change. The biggest lie of and about austerity is that 'there's not enough money'. That is untrue. We live in a world, gifted by God as Christians say, which has more than enough resources to sustain us – if we look after it, share it, and care for one another well. In fact it is not austerity but *generosity* that makes the world go round, and when we realise this we can genuinely begin to live well and to deconstruct the myths around the idea that the problem we face is a shortage which can only be addressed by cutting back.

Now some parts of the world do face huge shortages, of course. That is in significant part because they are denied resources or the wherewithal to get them by those whose interests monopolise decision-making. That involves the loss of billions of pounds that could be flowing to poor countries through a fair trading system and the fair finance which is denied to them, for example.

For others, like those of us living in the sixth richest country on earth, many of the problems faced by people living with economic deprivation, living with chronic sickness or disability, without a stable and well-remunerated job, or facing major health challenges, are immeasurably worsened by decisions to cut support – even though most of those same people have contributed to society through taxes, work, volunteering, caring and in myriad other ways. They are neither getting what they need nor what they deserve. Instead, we are spending billions on illegal wars or on bailing out banks (for which, note, the money suddenly appears – you do not get an extra tax bill when those decisions are made). In short, our priorities are wrong, and our outlook is based on viewing the world through the prism of shortage and meanness, not abundance and generosity. As Gandhi famously said (as quoted again in one of the sessions that follows), there is indeed enough to meet all our needs, but not for all our greed.

INTRODUCTION

Lent: Living towards abundance

'I came that you might have life, and have it in abundance', Jesus tells his followers in John's Gospel. He is telling the truth. But whether we do live like that is up to us when we have the wherewithal – which if we work together, support one another, share, forgive, care and love, can be the case. In order for it to be the case, however, we need to recognise and love our neighbours in and as ourselves. The 'feast or famine?' question in the Old Testament was about how to cope in societies where the primary question was survival. The technological and economic means to move beyond subsistence to surplus-based flourishing on a sustainable basis simply did not exist. Today, those means do exist, so if the planet is being despoiled, people starve and the poorest are abandoned that is not a result of a lack of money or resources, it is a matter of choice. Cutting health care while investing in weapons of mass destruction is, likewise, a decision.

The Christian Gospel is about becoming the kind of people and the kind of communities that can make better choices because we have cultivated the character and virtues, based on the self-giving love of God we meet in Jesus Christ, to enable that to happen. It is a message of Good News. God is for us, the world is there for our flourishing, we can be constantly renewed by forgiveness and making a fresh start when we mess up. Divine love is stronger than wrongdoing and death – and ultimately this, not power or money or force – is what our security and possibility is based on.

Lent is a time when we have a chance to reassess our priorities. It gives us the opportunity to try to remove bad habits and bad choices, and instead to make healthy decisions about living hopefully, generously and in solidarity with others near and far, in spite of all that the difficulty of living can throw at us. Rightly understood, Lent is not about austerity and meanness, but the discipline required to live abundantly. It is organising ourselves and being renewed so that the Feast of Life to which the Gospel invites us can be a reality for all, not something restricted to a few. Famine and austerity are not destiny. The love of God that overflows and is unconstrained: that is destiny. It is out of that spirit that we should be looking to reset our lives economically and in other ways, starting with the small choices and opportunities, but also speaking and working into the large ones. That is partly what Ekklesia exists to promote.

Reassessing our talents: who wins and loses

This brings us back to the parable of the talents in Matthew 25, the final verses of which lie so far unaddressed at the very beginning of this chapter. The tale is of a demanding lord who sets his servants a task, rewards those who make him rich, and punishes the one who most spectacularly fails to do that by not gaining interest on the lord's investment. Conventionally, people tend to assume that the lord in the story must be God. But that is rather puzzling, because the lord here is a greedy and unappealing figure who acts out of self-interest, not mercy.

That should be a clue that we have got the meaning of the story quite wrong. Jesus' original audience would have instantly recognised that this lord is most definitely not the God of Jesus. He is a harsh potentate who wants to 'harvest where I have not sown and gather where I have not scattered seed'. There is not an ounce of generosity to this master. His economic strategy, in fact, is to exact punitive interest from lending. However, the Jewish Law forbade usury, and it is not something Jesus endorses. On the contrary, he most frequently tells his followers to give to the poor without expecting return – a gift economy, not one based on extortion.

So Jesus' audience would immediately have got the point that the lord in this parable is not God, and not like Jesus. In fact, he is the opposite of the way, life and truth commended by Jesus. So this story is not an endorsement of ruthless economic exploitation, but a *warning against it.* Jesus is the Lord who turns earthly lordship, based on domination, upside down. The title his followers give him puts him in conflict with the lordly claims of Caesar, with an exploitative landlord system, and with the turning of the Temple into the court of a 'den of thieves' (Matthew 21:13) occupied by merchants and moneychangers.

In contrast to the Lord of Austerity, who declares that 'Whoever does not have, even what they have will be taken from them', Jesus offers abundant life, not based on acquisition, but donation. He also creates a community of the dispossessed who invest in solidarity not the stock market (the Beatitudes), and he dramatises the hope of a kingdom which in fact looks much more like a commonwealth of many mansions. In God's realm, indeed, there is an endless Feast of Life to which the excluded are given a place of priority and honour. The last shall be first. Such is the economy of God.

If this is so, then Christians and others of goodwill with whom we ally, should be seeking a path that is very different from the kind enshrined in the ideology of austerity – where the rich get richer, the bankers are bailed out, and those with least are hit hardest. Instead we need a modern economy characterised by mutuality, cooperation, generosity, community, sharing, sustainability and equity. That's miles from where things are at present, but change is possible. Churches and other civic groups can model different ways forward

– for example with the ecumenical Churches' Mutual Credit Union (http://cmcu.org.uk). Looking at the bigger picture, Daniel Christian Wahl says:

> *Ultimately, we need to transform finance and shift the flow of investment capital to perpetuate a Regenerative Economy that serves humanity and is a steward of Earth's ecosystems. […] The transition to a Regenerative Economy is about seeing the world in a different way – a shift to an ecological world view in which nature is the model. The regenerative process that defines thriving, living systems must define the economic system itself.* (https://medium.com/@designforsustainability/towards-a-regenerative-economy-bf1c2ed6f792)

Another way of framing matters, which Ekklesia is committed to working towards, is what John Gillibrand in his chapter, 'Beyond the Good Samaritan', calls the Caring Economy. This is about making the fundamental and mutual (not one-way) human activity of guarding our common fragility the basis for regenerative investment, alongside green technology for a post-carbon economy, and other priorities. A Caring Economy starts by recognising what the austerity mentality cannot – that the activity of caring (which we will almost all need to give and receive at some point in our life-cycles) is not a liability that needs to be cut out in order to 'save money', but a benefit to be invested in for human flourishing. Caring has the capacity to involve and engage the whole of society. But it needs an economic model, forms of social enterprise (in which faith and civic communities can play a potentially significant role) and the appropriate underpinning by good local and national government to make it work effectively for the common good.

Beyond austerity: the hope of the Gospel

So there is hope. But, meanwhile, we are left with the task of resisting, redirecting and resetting an austerity mindset, ideology and policy frame (it is all three) that is pointing us in the wrong direction. That remains the case in spite of some pre-emptive talk about 'the end of austerity' after the 2017 General Election and the Grenfell fire shock, which showed just how badly cuts were weakening our protective infrastructure, especially for the poorest.

This resistance, redirection and resetting of an austerity outlook is achieved not simply by political engagement – which should be about calling power to account, not indulging in party posturing – but by telling a different story about ourselves, our communities and the world. This is what the Gospel calls us to. It takes a narrative that spells doom for the human condition and rearranges it into an invitation to join a project of rescue and reorientation (of the kind Lent gives us a periodic opportunity to consider).

For example, Jesus is often quoted as saying 'the poor you will always have with you'? The context was in response to those who were dismissing a woman who had covered his feet in expensive perfume, an act of reckless generosity. Her religious critics said, hoping to gain favour with him, that she could have spent the money on the poor instead – not noticing that she was not far off that category herself. Jesus defended her uncalculated act of love for the true spirit it embodied. Imagine a world where we did that kind of thing for each other? Then he pointed her critics back to the reality of the responsibility that undoubtedly remained, towards those who are least, lost and last. But there is a twist. Again, his hearers would know that this saying about the poor always being with us was from Deuteronomy 15:11. There it is accompanied straightaway by the injunction: 'Therefore I command you to be openhanded toward your fellow Israelites who are poor and needy in your land' (rather than indulging in fatalism). Even more significantly, it is prefigured by a promise that if people turn around and develop a new way of life then the 'always' can be taken away, as in Deuteronomy 15:4: 'However, there need be no poor people among you, for in the land the Lord your God is giving you as your inheritance, God will richly bless you.'

In this context, Jesus' message is not one of passive acceptance of poverty. It is instead openly welcoming of beneficent extravagance (this woman was literally 'living beyond her means' to show the generosity she did). It is also tirelessly committed to acts of continuing service, and it highlights in the midst of this dramatic episode the practical hope of a different and better way. That is what we should be seeking too. Not accommodation to the pessimism of austerity, but a renewal of purpose to move in a different direction in matters small and large. That is what this course invites us to entertain during and well beyond Lent.

> *God of uncalculating love*
> *Whose heart overflows with laughter*
> *and whose hands gift life and liberation,*
> *May we show that same expansive and engaged*
> *generosity*
> *to all whose paths we cross*
> *that they may find at those intersections*
> *places of feasting and not of famine.*
> *Amen.*

COURSE GUIDANCE AND STRUCTURE

Each of the sessions in this book can be used for a period of personal or family reflection and prayer, or alternatively for an organised group session. The guidance below is intended to provide an adaptable framework for group use. It initially assumes a group of between five and a dozen people in a comfortable and hospitable environment, preferably beginning and/or ending with refreshments and social time. There are suggestions for larger groups at the end. For background reading on what austerity is, and a personal and biblical response to it, see the Introduction (especially) and the Afterword. Further resources are also provided at the end of the book. Additional online material is available at www.ekklesia. co.uk/lent2018.

Time Allocation

We suggest a maximum of two hours per session, including social time, and a minimum of an hour and a half. If it is an evening meeting, that might be 6pm to 7.30pm or 8.00pm, say; or 7pm to 8.30pm or 9pm; or 8pm to 9.30pm or 10pm, etcetera. A later start might suggest that people have had time to eat at home or in transit beforehand. An earlier start might necessitate the offering of snacks alongside liquid refreshment. It can be good to serve tea or coffee at the beginning, and allow that to spill over into the early stages of the session. Food is often best served at the end, unless you are starting late. That way things can feel less rushed and distracted.

In either event, the actual study session time set out below is an hour and 20 minutes. There's nothing to stop you going longer, but experience suggests that there is a law of diminishing returns in such matters. It is also often better leaving people wanting more (they can talk afterwards, or on another occasion, or use this book personally) rather than leaving them with indigestion!

The Leader and the Participants

Choose someone who will feel comfortable in the role – which means welcoming and well prepared (they have studied the material themselves, sent out pre-reading if desired, made sure they have any necessary materials, and are confident about keeping time without making people feel too pressed). The leader is not expected or required to 'have all the answers'. The idea is to pool insights and comments from the group. For discussion times, if you divide the time available by the number of people in the room, you will have a decent idea of what a fair allocation of the time would look like.

The leader is there to create an atmosphere where everyone is enabled to participate as they wish, and to guard against just a few people dominating proceedings. This may require a certain amount of diplomacy. It can really help if you gently say to someone beforehand, 'I know you'll have a lot of good insights to contribute, but I'm concerned some others might feel a bit reticent, so I'd really appreciate if you could help me make some space for them.' If there is food and drink to be served, it's good to have a host to do that, so that the group leader is not trying to multi-task.

Preparation

Each member of the group would definitely benefit from having a copy of this book. Some will want to go through the session on their own before coming to a group. Others will want to read more afterwards. Everyone could benefit from having read the key biblical passage (at the beginning of each chapter), the 'Gospel in Context' notes and the 'Reflection' before they come along. The most important one of these is the 'Reflection', because that is around 1,500 to 2,000 words, so in most cases will be a little long to read to the whole group. If necessary, make sure everyone gets a copy of the 'Reflection' a few days before the session, or even the complete set of five in advance. Time will be allocated for catch-up reading in the session, but pre-digestion would be best.

The biblical reading and 'Gospel in Context' commentary, which links the reading to the reflection, should be read aloud in the group. It is good to get different people to do different readings or prayers, so that a variety of voices are heard. Get people to agree beforehand or at the beginning, being sensitive to those who might need more warning than others.

In terms of materials: we suggest that you have pens and paper for everybody to take notes, and a flip chart, whiteboard or overhead projector with pens for the discussion sessions.

Make sure that people with sight or hearing difficulties are adequately included by provision of equipment or assistance before, during and after the session. Make sure that you use an accessible home or venue for people with wheelchairs and other physical needs.

Each chapter has any specific 'Leader's Guidance' for that session included at the top of the second page of the chapter.

Session Format

We suggest that you follow the same format and timing for each session. Here is an outline for adaptation as you wish. If you are pressed for time it is better to leave something out than try to rush. Attempting to do these sessions in an hour or less will most likely make it seem hurried. If you want to stretch the core session time from one hour and 20 minutes to an hour and a half, that would be fine. Go longer only if people are known to be really keen, or demand it! The pattern that follows consists of 35 minutes during which time people receive and consider personally three readings: a short biblical excerpt, a commentary, and then a reflection on the core topic. That is the first part of the session. It can be extended by five minutes or so if you want the reflection read aloud, rather than quietly (with or without a summary). The second part of the evening is 45 minutes for discussion, digestion and prayer. If you do add time, that is invariably where it will go.

HOSTING TIME (15 minutes)

It's good to do these as people arrive. The leader should know everyone's name. Coffee, tea or other suitable refreshments are good to have at the beginning, especially if people have been travelling or have needed to come straight from other activities. If people can be encouraged to get their drink and then take their place, that will assist a prompt start – as will advertising an arrival time ten or 15 minutes before you actually *want* to start. Getting people to sit in a circle is always good. Have Bibles and copies of this book available as required. Make sure any refreshment refills are on-hand and that people know where the necessary facilities are.

PART ONE: READING

WELCOME AND INTRODUCTIONS
(10 minutes)
Begin the evening by welcoming everybody. For the first night, the Foreword provides a simple introduction to the course. Get everybody to go quickly round and say their name and where they are from. (Use name labels or badges if it feels appropriate. This saves people the embarrassment of forgetting names.)

BIBLICAL READING (5 minutes)
This is printed on the first page of every session, usually from the Biblica (New International Version, NIV) online (http://www.biblica.com/bible/online-bible/). Another version can be substituted if you prefer. Allow a time of brief silence for digestion after the reading.

GOSPEL IN CONTEXT (5 minutes)
This offers some comment on both the issues that underlie the 'Reflection' that follows, and some linkage with the biblical passage. It is best not to get into discussion at this point. There is time provision for this later on.

REFLECTION (10 minutes)
This reading provides a 'thought for the day' (or afternoon, or evening!) on the core session topic. It

has been written from a personal angle provided by one of our Ekklesia associates. It should have been circulated beforehand – but allow up to ten minutes for people to read it quietly at the session, before moving on. Alternatively, you might give people a few minutes to read and then ask someone who has read it beforehand to highlight what for her are some key points from the 'Reflection' in two or three minutes.

PART TWO: DIGESTING

This follows a regular three-fold format: Commenting, Challenging, and Committing. The suggestion is that you handle this as follows.

COMMENTING (25 minutes)
Each chapter session will include specific prompts and ideas. Broadly, what stood out for people from the readings (light bulb moments)? What questions arose? What new insights have we gained?

CHALLENGING (10 minutes)
Are there one or two action points, personal or collective, for the church and/or for the community that come out of the readings and your discussion? That is, issues to be researched, service or advocacy activities to be engaged, lobbying to be done, or further conversation to be promoted?

COMMITTING (10 minutes)
A short time of prayer at the end, led by one or two people from the group and ending, if you wish, with the 'Collect' – and The Grace. ('The grace of our Lord Jesus Christ, the love of God and the friendship of the

COURSE GUIDANCE AND STRUCTURE

Holy Spirit be with you now and for evermore. Amen.') You might wish to use the Prayer of Jesus (The Lord's Prayer, or Our Father) too. There is additional prayer material towards the end of the book, which can be adapted for personal or group use. This is rendered in inclusive language.

This marks the end of the formal session.

Social Time and Food
(another 30 minutes or so)
If you are only allowing for an hour and a half time in total, you will not have time for this. If you are allowing for two hours in total, the ten minutes host time at the beginning and the hour and 20 minute session will mean that you have half an hour left for some snacks and socialising. This is obviously entirely flexible.

Larger Group Suggestion
One idea would be to combine 'Comment' and 'Challenge', and to split into smaller groups based either around pre-prepared questions (including some included in the five chapter sessions) or around questions or issues from the readings suggested by plenary feedback and collected by the leader on a flipchart. A time for 'reporting back' and an allowance for action suggestions can be incorporated. A decent timing of the three parts of this discussion time might be (for a group of, say, 30 in five groups of six): approximately 15 minutes in plenary, 20 minutes in groups and 15+ minutes feeding back. Allowing for overrun and a few minutes to get to and from groups, for which spaces would have been pre-allocated, the total time for the larger group discussion would be an hour, rather than 35 minutes for a small group that

stays together. You can allocate to groups by giving people a number on their chair when they arrive. The total session time for a larger group is likely to be an hour and 45 minutes, therefore, plus whatever social and refreshment time is allowed around that.

Additional Possibilities

The introductory chapter, 'Moving Beyond Austerity: A Christian Challenge', contains a substantial account of what austerity is and what a Christian alternative to it would begin to look like. It is organised into six sessions and could therefore provide the basis for an additional, preliminary or follow up course. The material in the Afterword, 'Beyond the Good Samaritan' is also eminently adaptable for study purposes.

WEEK ONE

Spending or Saving?
(Our part in the economy)

Jesus said to them, 'Watch out! Be on your guard against all kinds of greed; life does not consist in an abundance of possessions.'

And he told them this parable: 'The ground of a certain rich man yielded an abundant harvest. He thought to himself, "What shall I do? I have no place to store my crops."

'Then he said, "This is what I'll do. I will tear down my barns and build bigger ones, and there I will store my surplus grain. And I'll say to myself, 'You have plenty of grain laid up for many years. Take life easy; eat, drink and be merry'."

'But God said to him, "You fool! This very night your life will be demanded from you. Then who will get what you have prepared for yourself?"'

'This is how it will be with whoever stores up things for themselves but is not rich toward God.'

(Luke 12:14-18)

Leader's Note

As this is the first session, you might want to do a summary of what the course is about (see Foreword) and where it is going (outline the five sessions) at the beginning. The Introduction to this book provides an overview of what austerity is, what its impact is, and why it is a concern for Christians. This session raises practical questions about where, why and how spending and saving can be beneficial or otherwise. But it is primarily looking at the kind of attitude and worldview which can sustain different, more generous and creative financial and economic practices by Christians and others of goodwill. Session planning details are outlined in detail in the 'Course Guidance and Structure' chapter.

Gospel in Context

Should we spend or should we save? If so, how much? What will we spend on or what will we save for? Such basic, everyday decisions are one of the pillars of our economy – the treasury of goods, resources and trading symbols (money) that we keep hearing about on the news and reading about in the papers or on the Internet. These daily decisions that we make are crucial to ourselves and to others. They both shape, and are shaped by, what gets produced in the wider economy. In a market-led society they support or undermine things like fair trade and environmental protection by putting resources in one place and withholding them elsewhere.

The consumer pressure for low prices, for example, may be at the expense of rural producers, workers' wages, health (long hours, fast food) and the ecology (carbon industries). To put it another way, the aggregate demand created by our individual decisions has a big effect on larger outcomes and on where wealth ends up.

One issue facing Christians and others of good will, therefore, is about how to spend and save in ways that make the best use of our resources not just for our own benefit, but for the benefit of our neighbours near and far, and the planet which is God's gift to us all. Accounting for our use of resources can be a complex business, but at its heart the way we operate economically – as families, communities and as a society – is shaped by who we are and how we choose to live.

Followers of Christ are constantly enjoined in the Gospels to live generously and simply. We are reminded that all we have is a gift, and that the reciprocity of giving, not the building of barns for hoarding, is the way goods are to be multiplied and shared in the economy of God. Austerity is based on the belief that there is not enough to go round, so spending on public good and social support must be cut back. The Christian message invites us to look at things another way. If we give we shall receive and all will be able to share.

Similarly, Gandhi once famously said that there is enough on Earth for everybody's need, but not enough for everybody's greed. We might consider putting that differently today – there is plenty to meet our needs (which are for company, creativity and celebration, not just 'stuff'), but the plenty will turn to want if some are simply allowed to hoard, despoil and waste on an industrial scale at the expense of others.

But before thinking, praying and acting on some of those demanding issues and choices, lets reflect on the generosity and simplicity which can give us the personal, social and spiritual resources to put them in a fresh context.

Reflection:
Living generously and simply –
Jill Segger

Let me start with an observation by former banker and economic thinker Frances Coppola. She reminds us that, contrary to what much of what our culture encourages us to think, 'Our economy runs on generosity.' Coppola continues:

> *Everything we have, we have because of the generosity of others – the people who produce what we invent, buy what we produce, give us their time, their effort, their talents and – one way or another – their money. I call it generosity, though it goes by other names too: 'spending', 'producing', 'consuming', 'donating', 'helping'. Wealth is created by doing things for others. Doing things primarily for yourself may also benefit others – this is what my parents call 'enlightened self-interest', though we also know it as 'trickle-down economics'. But too often doing things primarily for yourself impoverishes both you and others: you, because self-centredness cuts you off from the richness of human interaction, and wealth is no substitute for love; and others, because your*

greed deprives them of wealth and your selfishness deprives them of your company. Selfishness and greed don't just cause poverty, they ARE poverty.
(Coppola Comment, 'Generosity', 20 October 2015)

Lent is a season in which we have the opportunity to develop personal and social practices that point us away from greed and towards generosity. But what does that mean and how shall we approach it? I am a member of the Religious Society of Friends (Quakers), which does not order its worship by a liturgical calendar. For three and a half centuries, we have held to a belief once known as 'A Testimony against times and seasons'. *Quaker Faith and Practice*, our book of guidance, explains it thus:

Another testimony held by early Friends was that against the keeping of 'times and seasons'. We might understand this as part of the conviction that all of life is sacramental; that since all times are therefore holy, no time should be marked out as more holy; that what God has done for us should always be remembered and not only on the occasions named Christmas, Easter and Pentecost.

In the worshipping life of our community, this may mean that a Friend finds themselves prompted by the Spirit to give a ministry (that is, to speak during Meeting for Worship) regarding the Nativity on midsummer's day or to reflect upon the meaning of Pentecost at New Year. So it is that Lent, understood as six weeks of self-denial observed in the early spring, has no formal hold on our imagination, tradition or spiritual lives.

But what *does* have a continual and profound influence on our manner of living is the Testimony to Simplicity. Quaker Testimonies are not doctrinal definitions, nor do they exist in any prescriptive or proscriptive forms. They are rather an attempt, which both differs and evolves in every culture and generation, to put into practice values that are central to our faith.

Simplicity is essentially the discipline of standing back from what Quakers of my parents' generation called 'cumber'. This refers to whatever is permitted to accumulate to the detriment of our spiritual lives. It is not confined to the pursuit and amassing of physical possessions: the concept also encompasses the blunting of our awareness of God and neighbour through failure to distinguish between desire and need. It is not a joyless puritanism which frowns on pleasure or sees the occasional treat as a spiritual failing – it is rather a matter of discernment as to the pull which consumerism, status, acquisition and self-righteousness may exercise over us throughout our lives if we are not alert to the needs of others.

But simplicity, properly understood, asks us to go further. It propels us towards engagement with Jesus' challenge to embrace radical *generosity*: 'if anyone would take your tunic, let him have your cloak as well.' (Matthew 5:40). Not only does this cut across our sense of possession, it confronts us with a material-based and meritocratic concept of security and rights. It demands that we respect the question asked of us.

To say 'Why should I give you my things? Get your own clothes', cuts us off from the liberating and transforming potential of generosity. The 'scrounger' versus 'hard-working families' rhetoric has taken root in popular thinking and in its underlying appeal to indignation, it divides and desensitises us as human beings made in the image of God. Here we may see the destructive nature of austerity as it plugs into something smaller dwelling within us, something that will brook no thoughtful pause, self-questioning humility or spur to enlargement.

Those who 'ask' through the welfare system are increasingly portrayed as undeserving and fecklessly 'feeling entitled', as people deficient in backbone and industry. We are encouraged to see them as deserving of punishment for being unable to conform to more righteous standards. In this moral landscape, the sanctioning of benefits for not having applied for sufficient jobs in one week to satisfy the Department of Work and Pensions, or for failing to keep a Job Centre appointment because of poor mental health, is presented to us as the *quid pro quo* of the right-thinking economy of the virtuous.

This mindset, which finds justification for turning away from desperate people who, in the world's sixth largest economy, are driven to food banks, or who are unable to keep their homes warm, is a good point at which to consider the strangely disconcerting parable of the vineyard workers told in Matthew chapter 20. What causes most of us to stumble is the sheer generosity of the Divine here portrayed.

> *The workers who were hired about five in the afternoon came and each received a denarius. So when those came who were hired first, they expected to receive more. But each one of them also received a denarius. When they received it, they began to grumble against the landowner. 'These who were hired last worked only one hour', they said, 'and you have made them equal to us who have borne the burden of the work and the heat of the day.'*
>
> *But he answered one of them, 'I am not being unfair to you, friend. Didn't you agree to work for a denarius? Take your pay and go. I want to give the one who was hired last the same as I gave you. Don't I have the right to do what I want with my own money? Or are you envious because I am generous?'*

Our concepts of fairness and of merit are overset here by the non-transactional generosity of God's nature. To conform ourselves to the turning-the-world-upside-down economy of the Commonwealth of Heaven, to be generous as God is generous, may take a little practice. A lot, even. And that is where simplicity comes into its own.

Advices and Queries, a small handbook of challenge, exhortation and insight which has evolved over the centuries to combine what is eternal with the changing, lived experiences of Friends, and which is perhaps the nearest thing Quakers have to a catechism, reminds us that 'a simple lifestyle, freely chosen, is a source of strength'. This is our spiritual, intellectual and emotional circuit training for conforming ourselves to the paradoxical and transformative, to disciplining ourselves away from the right-thinking place markers of free market capitalism and – let it be said – the less compassionate aspects of the so-called Protestant work ethic.

The free choosing is significant. Too many of our fellow citizens have next to no choice and their lifestyles are marked by deprivation, humiliation and despair. Simplicity is not a passing *de haute en bas* excursion into the sufferings of poverty from which one may return with a security-based glow of virtue from having taken a temporary plunge into the unfamiliar and disturbing. Nor is it an exercise in spiritual athletics, in the superiority of being more-ascetic-than-thou. Without an understanding of its purpose in fitting us for the ongoing and often unspectacular service of love, it is meaningless: as much a Sunday-supplement display of refined sensibility in a vulgar world as a tax evader's choice of an Amish kitchen.

The eighteenth-century American Quaker John Woolman urged his contemporaries to 'look upon our treasures, the furniture of our houses, and our garments, and try whether the seeds of war have nourishment in these our possessions.' This remains an excellent guide to self-awareness and mutuality in a society which has become adept at punishing those who have the least.

Simplicity and generosity in a consumer culture is a life's work and it is only in making it a habit of life that we may gradually learn to move away from the destructive polarities of feast or famine towards the generosity and sharing revealed to us as the way to the indwelling of the Divine and to justice for all.

Frances Copolla again, writing in a different register, observes:

> Humans are, as a species, innately wealthy. We are intelligent, resourceful and creative. And when times are good, we are generous. But when times are hard, our concern for others is often diminished due to our fear for our own future, and we withhold from others all that we have to offer.
>
> This is natural and perhaps understandable, but it is neither morally right nor economically sensible. When we

withhold our natural wealth from others, we do not keep it safe – we destroy it. Ideas that never become reality are worthless... When we fear scarcity, we create poverty.

I would add that simplicity, which I have exposited as the gateway to generosity, is one of four Quaker Testimonies. The others are peace, equality and truth. If I were to pose myself and others a Lenten challenge, it would be to examine the inseparable, interdependent nature of these pillars of our common life as children of one Father and Mother.

SESSION ONE

Commenting

This is a time for open discussion, inviting people to respond both to the biblical reading and commentary, and to the reflection. Start by asking people to identify points that particularly struck them as significant or important, and any flashes of inspiration or new insight ('light bulb moments').

Some questions for consideration:

- Luke 12 seems to contrast hoarding wealth with 'being rich towards God'. What might this tell us about God, and the different kind of wealth Christian fellowship and journeying with Christ opens us up to?

- In what ways do we see hoarding and the amassing of untouchable wealth going on in our society? What challenges and problems does this pose? What is to be done about it?

- Our true wealth is company, creativity and celebration – not accumulating money and possessions for their own sake? Discuss. What might his mean for you?

- 'Everything we have, we have because of the

generosity of others', says Frances Coppola. Think of examples from your own life and community. How might this insight change our attitude to those our culture is liable to think of as 'less deserving' or 'undeserving'?

- In Jill Segger's reflection, what is the relationship between generosity and simplicity, and how are the two related?

- In what ways might it be appropriate to 'live beyond our means' for the sake of the Gospel in a world of injustice and inequality?

- 'At its heart the way we operate economically – as families, communities and as a society – is shaped by whose we are and how we choose to live.' What difference can and should belonging to the company of Christ make to the way we make financial decisions?

- 'Austerity is based on the belief that there is not enough to go round, so spending on public good and social support must be cut back. The Christian message invites us to look at things another way. If we give we shall receive and all will be able to share.' Discuss. (You will also find material in the Introduction to help with this.)

Challenging

The Iona Community (https://iona.org.uk) is one dispersed Christian community which has, as part of its commitment, an 'economic discipline'. Members account to one another for their use of finance, resources and time – as well as looking critically at their carbon footprint, with a view to reducing it. Alongside that they commit to work prayerfully for justice and peace, to advocate with and for the poor, and their family groups pool some money to invest in public good.

- What practices could you and your church develop in beginning to commend generosity and simplicity as the bases for a better way of living, economically?

- How can churches make economic choices to directly assist the victims of austerity policies (those on low incomes, the jobless or people in precarious employment, disabled and sick people, those living in poverty, lone parents and others)?

- To what extent is this about assistance, and to what extent is it about advocating for policies that benefit rather than punishing the least well off? How does this relate to St Augustine's comment that 'charity is no substitute for justice withheld'? (See the Foreword.)

- 'Saving' can be about hoarding, to the detriment of others and ourselves. Yet good saving schemes for people with fewer resources (Credit Unions, rather than loan sharks) are vital, and combatting the huge problem of private debt is really important. How can good saving reinforce good spending?

- Spending to put resources into public good is beneficial for the wider economy and individuals, argue many economists who are critical of the austerity model, because it generates cycles of virtue (jobs, homes, green technology, further investment, etc.) Could church investments be improved by thinking more about that opportunity? How?

Committing (Prayer)

Jesus our incarnate brother
Who gave without reserve but also withdrew into
    quietness,
Help us to learn from your example
that we too may spend and be spent wisely and
    well
within the economy of your Commonwealth.
Amen.

WEEK TWO
Hunger or Satisfaction?
(Food poverty and consumption)

One of those at the table with him said to Jesus, 'Blessed is the one who will eat at the feast in the Kingdom of God.'

Jesus replied: 'A certain man was preparing a great banquet and invited many guests. At the time of the banquet he sent his servant to tell those who had been invited, "Come, for everything is now ready."

But they all alike began to make excuses. The first said, "I have just bought a field, and I must go and see it. Please excuse me."

Another said, "I have just bought five yoke of oxen, and I'm on my way to try them out. Please excuse me."

Still another said, "I just got married, so I can't come."

The servant came back and reported this to his master. Then the owner of the house became angry and ordered his servant, "Go out quickly into the streets and alleys of the town and bring in the poor, the crippled, the blind and the lame."

"Sir," the servant said, "what you ordered has been done, but there is still room."

Then the master told his servant, "Go out to the roads and country lanes and compel them to come in, so that my house will be full."'
(Luke 14:15-23)

Leader's Note

Following the previous session, which featured a quite personal look at generosity and simplicity as the driving forces of an alternative life stance to austerity, this session begins to address the very real consequences of the cutbacks and sanctions operated in Britain in recent years. The reflection looks at the bridge between compassionate service and the quest for justice in society so that the wounds too many now endure can be addressed structurally. Session planning details are outlined in detail in the 'Course Guidance and Structure' chapter.

Gospel in Context

The Kingdom (or Commonwealth) of God is portrayed in the Gospels as a joyous feast. But who gets invited to that feast, and how? Jesus' followers and co-religionists wanted to know. Some among the religious authority figures of his day thought they knew the answer. The 'respectable' and 'deserving' were the only ones who could sup with God. They obeyed the Law, were ritually pure, and attended properly to their duties in life. The parable of the feast in Luke 14 is about those very people. They duly get their invitation, but they have far too many other things going on in life to give it proper attention. So the 'certain man' (yes, he would have been male!) in the story decides instead to invite the marginal, the scruffy and the impure – those who in conventional terms would be unworthy of an invitation.

The message of Jesus is clear. If even an earthly potentate could end up including the uninvited (and turning away those of the 'right' status in verse 24), how much more will the God he called 'Abba' make sure that the table is full, with priority given to those the world often casts aside? This message is echoed throughout the Gospels. Mary's Song, the Magnificat, is about God 'exalting the humble and weak' and 'turning the rich away, empty'. Jesus himself was accused of eating with sinners. At the end of Matthew's Gospel, in chapter 25, the warning in judgement includes the words, 'You saw me hungry, but you did not feed me' in reference to 'the least of these, my brothers and sisters'.

Our reflection this week is on not just the imperative to feed the hungry, but on addressing the reasons the hungry have no food – even in parts of the rich, industrial world. It doesn't make comfortable reading. But it is a reminder that the economy of God is not about money and accumulation, but people and communion. Is that not where our priorities should lie?

Reflection:
Hungry for food, hungry for justice – *Keith Hebden*

A young woman, Denise, with her toddler at her feet, is sitting in the church café. They are here for a handout from the local food bank. She is sitting with her dad and her partner, Dave. Her partner explains that he left his job because he was offered another job with better prospects and pay, but that after a two-week probationary period they decided to 'let him go'. Because he had, according to the regulations, 'voluntarily' quit a secure job,

Dave was sanctioned and all his money was stopped.

The first Dave's girlfriend knew of all this was when she went to the cash point. Her card was refused. The cupboards were empty and so now was the bank account. The pain and shame they all felt was great. Rather than receiving a hand up, the family had been slapped down and made even more insecure. Now they are forced to rely on charity for the food they and their child needs.

This is far from a lone story or example. A young man comes to our Anglican Evensong and tells us that he has a food parcel but no electricity on the meter. He is in arrears and cannot for the life of him work out whether to pay the bills or to get something to eat. Could we help?

A woman in one of the poorest estates in Leicester is told by her mum not to go to the local food bank, even though she needs help – in case she is seen. She has to walk two miles to another food bank so that she can lessen the shame of not being able to buy her own food again.

Most of us who work in inner cities, in outer estates and in an increasing number of rural locations can tell a host of other stories, similar to these. The number of food banks in the UK has shot through the roof in recent years. This is a practical response to a growing need. It is also a shocking indictment on the UK, which is the seventh richest nation on earth.

Recent figures from the Trussell Trust, a prominent Christian charity, show a two per cent increase in food bank use over the last year or so, with more than 1.1 million three-day emergency food supplies given to people in crisis by their network of 424 food banks in 2015/16 and beyond (https://www.trusselltrust.org/news-and-blog/latest-stats/).

The main reasons that people give for visiting a food bank are changes and delays to benefits or having an income too low to support oneself adequately. Often those whose benefits have been changed or cut are in work or are in and out of low-paid insecure work. They are part of what is often referred to as 'the precariat'; people living and surviving (just) in precarious circumstances shaped by forces well beyond their control – government policies, private investment decisions, international capital flows, and now the uncertainty of Brexit.

Food banks do an important job in meeting immediate needs. Some go further, as they incorporate additional services like debt advice, clothing banks, and signposting to other agencies. They can also offer community and emotional support for people. However, none of this stems the tide of increased hunger and destitution. Those who provide local charity at food banks or on soup kitchens are steam valves for a system that is creaking and under pressure – and which, in its willingness to allow some to accumulate unimaginable (often untaxed) wealth while others live in abject conditions, is clearly unjust from a Christian perspective.

The Hebrew prophet Amos, representatives of Muslim, Hindu, Sikh and other traditions, and many secular prophets – all have spoken out against a culture which tolerates want in the midst of plenty; which seeks to 'balance the budget' by cutting support for the poorest while bailing out the speculators, and which frequently blames those faced with the intolerable decisions of poverty – like the people we have been looking at in this session – for their plight.

Yes, we all have faults. But the cost of falling or failing is disproportionate for those who have almost nothing, while it can be shrugged off with relative ease by those living in comfort, and ignored by those with great affluence. There is something morally and systemically wrong here. Food banks are a clear sign and warning of this, if only we have eyes to see and ears to hear.

Occasionally, in the midst of a society in which inequality reigns, there is a visceral explosion on our streets. People with nothing to lose, or those who have been fed a diet of unrealisable expectation through the multi-million pound advertising industry, rebel. But mostly, thanks to the practical and pastoral responses of people of all faiths and of no religion but 'good faith', we manage to hold together a fragmented society under pressure. Without these steam valves, who knows what would happen? Countless lives have been saved and who can calculate how many uprisings, thefts of desperation, and relationship-breakdowns have been averted through works of mercy?

We cannot let things rest there, however. Sometimes we are all so busy being steam valves for unjust systems that it is easy to forget to be whistle-blowers too. Or as US evangelical social activist Jim Wallis likes to put it: we're great at pulling drowning people out of the river but not so good at going up stream to see who is pushing them in. Or as the Christian mystic Leo Tolstoy observed, there is a great deal of difference between setting up a hospital to bind the wounds of those who are being injured by an industrial society, and challenging those institutions who are tolerating (or even profiting from) the process that produces the injury.

So providing practical and pastoral assistance and challenging root injustice are two vital tasks. But how can we do both? The prophet Micah calls us to 'do justice, love mercy, and walk humbly with God'. How can we have time for justice while we're so busy with mercy? The answer is that we need to find creative ways to fit whistles onto the steam valves we build. People who visit food banks can be supported to write to their MP to tell their story and push for Living Wage initiatives and to challenge the impact of welfare changes that proceed without welfare compassion.

We need to build broad based community organisations that bring our institutions and agencies together (churches, faith groups and secular partners), both at a local level and nationally, in order to allow those who go hungry – and who hunger for justice – to speak for themselves. Advocacy by and with those at the 'cutting edge' is really important. Speaking for people without speaking to them can be patronising and unhelpful. As the famous South African saying has it (one adopted in Scotland and elsewhere by the Poverty Truth Commission): 'nothing that's about us, but without us, can be for us.'

For Christians living in suburban comfort that may mean forming new alliances with those they read about but do not meet – hidden in their own neighbourhoods, as well as more visible elsewhere. It is about relationship and respect leading to greater understanding, solidarity, and organising for change locally and beyond. 'Think locally, act globally', as another well-known aphorism has it. Groups like Church Action on Poverty, Ekklesia and others can provide resources, ideas and inspiration for the journey that needs to be made from feeding the hungry to satisfying the hunger for justice.

As an example, back in 2014 a group called End Hunger Fast brought together thousands of food bank users and volunteers as well as national leaders from various faiths, to fast in solidarity with those who are going hungry across Britain. Our national campaign, working with partners such as Trussell Trust and Church Action on Poverty, helped change the conversation on hunger in Britain at a time when it was the demonising of those who go hungry was in full media and political flow and led to an important conversation with the then Prime Minister.

An All Party Parliamentary Group (APPG) was then set up at Westminster to look into food poverty, although few of its recommendation have yet been realised. This demonstrates the need for continuing action and pressure. In 2016 an even wider alliance of agencies (including Church Action on Poverty, Child Poverty Action Group, FareShare, Magic Breakfast, Oxfam, Sustain and the Trussell Trust) launched 'End Hunger UK', as they invited us to continue to the important work of speaking truth to power and turning the world as it is into the world as it should be. This work continued into 2017 and beyond.

Moving from pastoral action to political action (in the sense of addressing the moral issue of power, rather than simply helping those who are the victims of its misuse) has its own challenges. The Catholic seer Dom Helder Camara, who worked in Recife in Brazil, once famously observed: 'When I feed the poor they call me a saint; but when I ask why the poor have no food, they call me a communist.'

Throughout the ages Christians have likewise been accused of being subversive when they challenge an unjust status quo in the name of the God who promises to 'make all things new'. But as people of faith and hope we cannot be content to only love mercy and walk humbly with our God; we must also do justice with our God. And God promises that those who hunger and thirst for righteousness will indeed be satisfied.

Last but not least, the Kingdom (or Commonwealth) of God is imaged in the Gospels as a huge feast in which all shall be satisfied. Food shared is at the very heart of Christian community. For Christians who celebrate specific sacraments, God comes to us in Christ through the medium of bread and wine, respectively the very stuff of life and the means to celebrate life.

It is an obscenity to share the food of heaven at the Eucharistic table without also working tirelessly to ensure that the hungry are fed, both here and throughout the globe. As the Orthodox remind us, 'communion after Communion' entails the service and advocacy that flows out beyond our sharing at God's table where we are knitted together in community.

In Britain today that surely involves doing everything we can not just to provide food to the hungry, but to challenge the seventh wealthiest country in the world at a structural, policy level to ensure that none go without the basic necessities of food, shelter, health and education.

Does this sound too 'political' or materialistic for Christians to be attending to? It is not. The Gospel is based on the fact that the Word Became Flesh, and that the Spirit testifies to the flesh as the place where God meets, greets, challenges and changes us. This redraws and dissolves the boundary between what is often regarded as 'material' and what is often regarded as 'spiritual'. All comes from, and is accountable to, God.

As Tolstoy again said: 'Food for myself is a material issue; food for my neighbour is a spiritual issue.'

SESSION TWO

Commenting

Again, this is where we have time for open discussion, inviting to people respond both to the biblical reading and commentary, and to the reflection. Start by asking people to identify points that particularly struck them as significant or important, and any flashes of inspiration or new insight ('light bulb moments').

Some questions for consideration:

- What is your reaction to the personal stories of food poverty recounted here? Do you know of other examples yourself? Why are some in touch with people who experience hunger in Britain, while many are not? How can the gap in understanding and commitment to action on food poverty be addressed?

- 'Food for myself is a material issue; food for my neighbour is a spiritual issue.' Discuss Tolstoy's claim in relation to the popular division that many make between 'the spiritual' and 'the material'. How does the Gospel challenge such a polarity, and what are the implications for our action as Christians and churches?

- Who are 'the uninvited' in your neighbourhood,

region and country? How do we make sure that policies on food, welfare, health and social care are driven by the experience and need of those currently excluded from the feast?

- The Gospel challenges all to repentance: to the turnaround in our lives that following Jesus creates and requires. What can and should that mean for addressing the big gap between the 'haves' and the 'have nots' in society? How can the church address its own economic gulf?

- How can work with food banks be linked to advocacy to address the systemic causes of food hunger?

- 'Our real charitable aim should be to abolish food banks by making them no longer necessary.' How can we go about this? http://lacuna.org.uk/food-and-health/the-foodbank-dilemma/

Challenging

End Hunger UK is a campaigning initiative that started with Christians and has now brought together people from a whole range of backgrounds, religious and otherwise. Its aim is simple: 'Everybody should have access to good food. Nobody should go to bed hungry.'

To spell that out in a little more detail: 'Our vision is to live in a country where everyone has access to good food and no one goes to bed hungry. Please add your voice to thousands of others, and help build a groundswell of pressure on politicians and government so that they take the issue of hunger in the UK seriously. Join the campaign and play your

part in ensuring that people don't go hungry for any reason.'

End Hunger UK is supported by many national organisations, including: Child Poverty Action Group; Church Action on Poverty; Ekklesia, FareShare; First Steps Nutrition; Food Ethics Council; Fabian Commission on Food and Poverty; The Food Foundation; Food Matters; Nourish Scotland; Sustain: the alliance for better food and farming; Trussell Trust; Independent Food Aid Network and Magic Breakfast.

- What can you and your church do to back the campaign against food hunger on our doorstep? Find out more at: http://endhungeruk.org

- Find out more about the issue of food waste in supermarkets and households. Can you take some simple steps to help address this scandal? Household food waste alone increased to 7.3 million tonnes in 2015, according to research published in 2017. https://www. lovefoodhatewaste.com/why-save-food

- Almost every UK supermarket has now responded in some way to consumer pressure and linked up with food redistribution organisations such as FareShare and Foodcycle.

  But while good practice is emerging, supermarkets' work with charities is barely denting the waste problem. FareShare estimates it accesses only two per cent of supermarkets' available food surplus. Much more needs to be done: http://www.fareshare.org.uk

- There is an important and disturbing relationship between benefit sanctions and food hunger. MPs need to be made aware of this and encouraged to change this http://endhungeruk.org/know-sanctions-foodbank-use/

Committing (Prayer)

Bread of Life,
You knew the pleasure of feasting with friends
but also the hard hunger of wilderness places.
May we never take more than we need
And always share what we have
That all may be satisfied.
Amen.

WEEK THREE
Health or Wealth?
(How we choose and make priorities)

A man with leprosy came to him and begged him on his knees, 'If you are willing, you can make me clean.'

Jesus was indignant. He reached out his hand and touched the man. 'I am willing,' he said. 'Be clean!' Immediately the leprosy left him and he was cleansed.

Jesus sent him away at once with a strong warning: 'See that you don't tell this to anyone. But go, show yourself to the priest and offer the sacrifices that Moses commanded for your cleansing, as a testimony to them.'

Instead he went out and began to talk freely, spreading the news. As a result, Jesus could no longer enter a town openly but stayed outside in lonely places. Yet the people still came to him from everywhere.
(Mark 1:40-45)

FEAST OR FAMINE?

Leader's Note

In this session we look further into who is suffering as a result of austerity policies that reduce public funds for public good. There is perhaps a surprising connection between the biblical reading from Mark's Gospel, which looks at how Jesus challenged an excluding system in his day, as well as focusing on the person and their needs, and concerns which need to be addressed in modern-day Britain. The commentary below makes that link. The reflection cites some of the research about the impact of austerity, but gives priority to human experience of what is going wrong and what needs to be done. The focus is on health and caring, raising questions about where our collective wealth is going (or not going). Session planning details are outlined in detail in the 'Course Guidance and Structure' chapter, as before.

Gospel in Context

The story of the healing of the leper in the first chapter of Mark's Gospel raises many questions. (Perhaps the most immediate one for the modern mind is, 'How can we believe that the touch of Jesus was able to restore health to a chronically sick person?' Suffice it to say that people's experience of God in the person of Christ seemed to produce all kinds of eruptions in the expected order of things. But it is clear from the denouement of this story that the reason Mark included it was because of the trouble Jesus was in.

After all, he was going around offering free, unauthorised health care. This was against the rules. It was certain recognised religious figures, operating within the Temple system (and its treasury) who were supposed to decide who was healed and on what conditions. The only condition Jesus recognised was need. He was indignant at the suffering of this man – which was not just about a disabling physical condition, but also about stigma, social isolation and exclusion from the community. The touch and presence of Jesus restored all that. Whereas he was probably not 'ritually clean'; enough to seek help from the religious healthcare system, Jesus' concern was not with the system and its spiritually-sanctioned austerity, but with the person

The bridge between the very different biblical era from which this story emerges and our own age lies in the question of priorities: who gets to access health and wellbeing, and on whose and what terms? Austerity politics and economics are cutting more people off from health, social care and social security – public goods, which figures like Archbishop William Temple struggled for long and hard. Jesus puts the restoration of people and community first. That's a challenge both to the church and to the society in which the church seeks to live out its followership of the Word Made Flesh.

Reflection:
A crisis for caring –
Savitri Hensman

As austerity has taken hold in the UK and beyond, increasing numbers of people have struggled to get the health and social care they need. There are plentiful facts and figures on the scale of the crisis but it is important to remember the personal impact in every case.

A Member of Parliament, Anna Turley, told the House of Commons, in a discussion about ambulance services in 2016:

'A 72-year-old woman in Marske in my constituency fell and fractured her hip in the street in the centre of the village. She was left lying in immense pain on the pavement in the freezing cold. It is a seaside town and she was left virtually on the sea front for three hours. Thanks to members of the public and many local business owners who came out of their shops, she was cared for by the community; but we can imagine not just her distress but the distress and horror of the community at seeing such a thing happening in their village.'

At the other end of the age spectrum, a crisis in child and adolescent mental health services means that numerous young patients for whom GPs are seeking help are turned away. 'Recently all referrals seem to get bounced. They've included children who self-harm, a child who was physically abusing his mother and a child with severe night terrors after the loss of his father. All of them were advised to contact local charitable organisations,' Dr Karen Cox in Bristol told *Pulse* magazine, when it was carrying out an investigation. Other reports, too, have pointed out the difficulties often faced by seriously ill young people in getting timely and adequate mental health treatment.

Social care users too have been finding it increasingly hard to get the support they require to lead independent lives or even meet their basic needs. Jennifer, responding to a Scope charity report on disabled people's experiences of social care, said:

'*I just survive. I'm lucky if I get two baths a week. I don't get hot food or drinks Monday to Thursday. I'm lucky if I manage to eat at all. I often don't get undressed and sleep in my clothes because it's easier. I sleep on a two-seat sofa downstairs so that I will make it to the loo. My house is not wheelchair accessible so I often have to crawl to the loo. This is not a life.*'

Lack of support can also lead to too heavy a reliance on family and friends, which affects them too. One carer told Carers UK, when it was preparing its *State of Caring UK* 2016 report, commented that, 'Less respite per year means having less quality time with my husband. Day care has been reduced so having to care for more hours, feeling tired and stressed.'

Staff too can be affected, including those who put in unpaid overtime to deal with their workload, and then get ill themselves. 'All staff including non-clinical based roles are under extreme pressure with many of us working c.60 hours per week on 37.5 hours contracts for no additional pay and still not keeping up', a head of midwifery told the Royal College of Midwives. Another said, 'I feel staff are feeling the pressure of austerity with the major drive to bring down costs within the NHS.'

Many of us will know others in similar situations or have experienced these ourselves.

The impact of austerity

In recent years, governments have made efforts to reduce the role of the state in addressing people's needs, while expanding market opportunities and freedoms for businesses. This has affected health and social care in three main ways: by driving up levels of ill health, cutting funding to services and causing disruption as the switch to private provision (often with built in profit for contractors) is pursued.

People's health may be damaged by their social and physical environment – for instance poverty, poor housing and working conditions, insecurity or violence – as well as factors such as lack of access to stop smoking, drug and alcohol services. So the cuts in social security support, job security, public services and legal aid have affected public health. At the same time, tax cuts and loopholes for large corporations and the wealthy, leading to displays of luxury in contrast to the hardship faced by those struggling to get by, can leave many feeling even worse.

In addition, if some then channel that into hostility towards their neighbours who are 'different' – for instance people who are migrants or minority ethnic, lesbian, gay, bisexual or transgender or disabled – health can be further undermined. Also people feeling disempowered in society may sometimes try to deal with this by aggressive or controlling behaviour towards family members or others, especially women.

Much is known about the impact of specific measures. For instance cuts in Pension Credit spending for worse-off pensioners have been found to have a significant link with a rise in death rates among those aged 85 or over from 2010-13, according to research published in the *Journal of the Royal Society of Medicine*.

In another study, published by the *British Medical Journal* (*BMJ*), Bristol University and other researchers listened to people who have self-harmed and mentioned job loss, economic hardship or the impact of austerity measures as a factor. One participant, 23-year-old 'Paul', explained:

'I had aspirations and stuff when I left school. I wanted to be an electrician. I went and did the courses and the rest of it and I applied for every apprenticeship within thirty miles of my house but ever since I was sixteen I've not even had one interview, not even a phone call or email back – no-one…. I felt like I was stuck in a rut and the drugs and the alcohol... I ended up feeling more and more worthless every time you get shot down. There's only so many times you can be defeated before you start to defeat yourself and eventually I think I

just got to that point where I'd had enough.'

Other research has looked at the overall effects. In an extended version of a *BMJ* editorial, Professor Danny Dorling wrote:

'On 3 June 2016, on the very the day the EU referendum was held, the UK's Office for National Statistics (ONS) released its latest annual mortality figures... An unprecedented rise in mortality was reported which was revealed to have risen across all the countries of the UK... By March it was becoming abundantly clear that deaths in the UK were rising and self-reported health quality had been falling year after year for some time, but as we did not have denominator populations we could not be sure that these changes were real changes in rates. Now we are sure... The underlying reason for worsening health and declining living standards was not immigration, but ever growing economic inequality and the public spending cuts'.

Secondly, lack of funding has put pressure on services and tightened rationing. This is especially noticeable because more people have been living to an age when health problems are common or, due to modern technology, have survived serious illnesses or accidents but with a need for ongoing care. Major shortfalls in NHS and local authority social services budgets have been reported, with cuts or long waits in frontline services.

When there are not enough staff on duty to care for hospital patients safely, or someone is denied a treatment they would have previously been offered, the impact is clear. Yet people may not find out what is happening, even in their own neighbourhood, until they are directly affected or a scandal is reported in the newspapers.

Thirdly, the push for privatisation means that money and time which could be spent on relieving suffering is spent on bids and lawyers. Services can be placed in the control of those with little experience and who may cut quality to increase profits. Some private providers try hard to keep up standards – but not all. This does not mean that all 'reforms' are bad – but some do seem to put company profits above patient care.

A faith perspective

Most people know from experience how unpleasant it can feel to be ill, even for a short time, and also to miss out on doing the things one enjoys or takes for granted. It can be frustrating to be out of action even briefly with an injury or stuck in traffic or on an unmoving train, distressing to feel intense emotional or physical pain even for a moment.

Hardly anyone would want to be in such situations themselves if this can be avoided. If Christians (and others) believe, 'In everything do to others as you would have them do to you' and 'You shall love your neighbour as yourself' (Matthew 7:1, 22:39), preventing or relieving suffering is important.

Jesus was well-known for healing the sick, for instance the woman suffering from constant bleeding for 12 years, a condition which also involved social isolation (Mark 5:25-34), and one of his best-known stories involves a traveller who comes to the aid of someone attacked and badly injured (Luke 10:29-37). He taught that those who visit the least of his brothers and sisters who are sick do so to him (Matthew 25:31-46).

One notion he challenged which was popular in his time, and still found today, was that being sick or injured was a sign of being more sinful than others (Luke 13:1-5, John 9:1-5). It can be tempting (partly because it can be uncomfortable to recognise how frail and at risk all humans are) to be judgmental towards those in poor health, but Jesus' advice 'Do not judge, so that you may not be judged' (Matthew 7:1-5) is worth noting. Indeed people sometimes behave unwisely, affecting their health, and healthy living should be encouraged. But without fully understanding someone's story, it is easy to jump to conclusions. If, say, someone had a traumatic childhood scarred by abuse, made a real effort to turn their life around, then started drinking again after being made redundant, simply blaming them is unhelpful.

The psalms sometimes paint a vivid

picture of what it can feel like to be ill (e.g. Psalms 88, 102) and, with the rest of Hebrew Scriptures, point out that widespread injustice affects health (e.g. Psalms 82, 94). In Christ's suffering and crucifixion, God enters at the deepest level into the world of vulnerable and mortal humans – and, in the resurrection, offers the hope of a new heaven and earth where pain and loss are no more.

But, importantly, in the Gospels God's Kingdom (or Commonwealth) is not simply postponed into the future, or treated as a 'life after life'. The Risen Christ is transformed, but still carries his wounds. He invites his followers into a movement for recognising and enacting God's Kingdom of transformed relationships and restored life here and now. To be baptised as a Christian is to become part of a 'new creation', which means that we cannot simply ignore the plight of those who are suffering, or 'leave it to God to sort out'.

In the company of Christ, the Word Made Flesh, we are called to stand in solidarity with all who suffer or who are oppressed now. This means acts of mercy, but also addressing the systemic wrong that we are confronted with personally and corporately. When we have a choice to make between money and people, people must come first. Mammon is a bad master. Our resources should be at the disposal of the healing of persons-in-community, not the other way round.

SESSION THREE

Commenting

This is a time for open discussion, inviting people to respond both to the biblical reading and commentary, and to the reflection. Start by asking people to identify points that particularly struck them as significant or important, and any flashes of inspiration or new insight ('light bulb moments'). This time the 'comment' is based around propositions rather than questions, though you may choose to come up with your own questions arising from the Bible reading, commentary and topic reflection.

Some issues for consideration:

- Christians are already often involved in caring for people who are sick or need support. This may be as part of a church or as a family member, volunteer or worker. At a time of austerity, such help may be especially valuable.

- There are other things too that can be done. What each person, congregation or group can do depends on their own situation and the other demands on their time and energy.

Actions may include:

- Listening attentively to people's experiences of health and care today – as patients, carers, friends and workers – in person and through local media, and trying to get a sense of the effects of cuts and other changes.

- Sharing one's own story if this feels safe, if personally affected: often in Christian and other communities, it can seem as if people affected by particular policies are 'out there', not those they know.

- Trying to be aware of our own feelings – for instance sadness, anger or helplessness – and assumptions.

- Trying to find out more about the causes of ill health or unwellness, and difficulty in accessing health and social care, and looking more deeply at the assertion that it is no longer practical to provide free healthcare to all, paid for through national insurance and other taxes, or social care to all who need it.

- Finding out about local and nationwide campaigns and perhaps getting involved.

Challenging

- Should Christians and other people of goodwill take action when the wealth of a few is given higher priority than the health and wellbeing of many others?

- Austerity has sharpened these choices for many, and in some cases has all but removed their choices altogether. For example, the poorest UK households are often locked out of the cheapest deals on energy and phone tariffs. Research by Citizens Advice in Scotland has suggested that people living in poverty pay on average 10 per cent more than others for essential goods and services, Insurance premiums are higher in poorer areas. Make-do loans from private lenders can be astronomically expensive when cheap credit arrangements are denied to those who are jobless and on low incomes. Healthier foods are more expensive. And so it goes on.

- The Church of Scotland, the Iona Community, the Scottish Episcopal Church and the Joint Public Issues Team (which includes some of the major Free Churches in the UK) have all spoken out about 'the poverty premium'. The Joseph Rowntree Foundation has identified it as a priority for 2017/18 and beyond. Look into what you can do to get these issues addressed: https://www.jrf.org.uk/blog/acting-unfair-poverty-premiums-must-be-2017-priority

Committing (Prayer)

God of the just measure
You hear the cry of widow and orphan
and see the smallest sparrow fall;
May we be so tuned to the song of your Kingdom
that all our choices always echo its chords
and complete its cadences.
Amen.

WEEK FOUR

Security or Insecurity?
(The burden on disabled people and the poorest)

So in everything, do to others what you would have them do to you, for this sums up the Law and the Prophets.
(Matthew 7:12)

'Come, you who are blessed by my Father; take your inheritance, the kingdom prepared for you since the creation of the world. For I was hungry and you gave me something to eat, I was thirsty and you gave me something to drink, I was a stranger and you invited me in, I needed clothes and you clothed me, I was sick and you looked after me, I was in prison and you came to visit me.'
Then the righteous will answer him, 'Lord, when did we see you hungry and feed you, or thirsty and give you something to drink? When did we see you a stranger and invite you in, or needing clothes and clothe you? When did we see you sick or in prison and go to visit you?'
The King will reply, 'Truly I tell you, whatever you did for one of the least of these brothers and sisters of mine, you did for me.'
(Matthew 25:34)

Leader's Note

Security or insecurity. Is it a choice? For too many, it isn't, frankly. In this session we hear some of their stories, and consider the macro decisions that deeply impact the choices people at the sharp end of life have, which can end up being life or death choices in the most difficult way. Here we bring the experience of people who are suffering under a seemingly unliftable burden into contact with a Gospel that asks us to reconsider our own attitudes and behaviour in the light of others, and which sets out in stark terms the responsibility we have before God to put the poorest and most vulnerable in society first. Welfare shouldn't just be a last ditch survival issue, it should be about how we all fare well – starting with those who really are living on the edge. Session planning details are outlined in detail in the 'Course Guidance and Structure' chapter.

Gospel in Context

How difficult it can be to see the world through someone else's very different experience. How easy it is to judge others, especially those less privileged and articulate than ourselves, those struggling to make ends meet, or people who provide a ready scapegoat for what worries or threatens us. While Jesus proclaims and lives an ethic of radical inclusion (giving his first concern to the last, the least and the lost), the Gospel also engages the common ethic of the Golden Rule, or 'do as you would be done by', in Matthew chapter 7. This provides a clear basis for collaborative action between Christians and those of other faiths or none ('people of good faith' – Canon Peter Challen) in addressing the poverty and dislocation exacerbated by austerity.

But Jesus goes further. The famous parable of the Last Judgment in Matthew chapter 25 calls the peoples and nations to account for how they have treated those pushed to the edges: the homeless, prisoners, the hungry. This is the moral basis upon which we are to assess our actions as believers, as faith communities and as a society. How has it lifted up those with least resources, those who are left out, and those who are suffering? Or to put it another way: in every decision about how power is being used (which is what 'politics' means, in its broad sense), the issue is always, 'Who wins, who loses and who decides?' (Brian Wren, *Education for Justice*, SCM Press)

Reflection:
Welfare means all faring well – *Bernadette Meaden*

Social security (now often referred to as 'welfare') can be seen as a very tangible expression of Christian principles explored elsewhere in this course. Archbishop William Temple and others in the earlier part of the twentieth century worked hard to seek reflected in social structure and public policy key principles that go to the heart of how people are to be treated in the light of the Gospel message – God's active desire for all to be brought into good and right relationship.

The idea is simple. Everybody who is able to contribute pays into a collective fund, and everybody who needs support thereby receives help from that fund. In this way, we look after each other across the wide range of personal, social, economic and health circumstances we face. By giving, we also receive – both individually, and as members of a society that recognises how the wellbeing of each is related to the wellbeing of all.

Across Britain, years of austerity, combined with a radical programme of changes to the welfare system, has had a dramatic impact on the social security system and on the lives of people who depend upon it. It has to a large extent removed security from the most vulnerable people in society.

The Centre for Welfare Reform (http://www.centreforwelfarereform.org) has calculated that spending cuts and social security changes have hit people in poverty (13 million people, according to the Joseph Rowntree Foundation) five times harder than the general population, disabled people nine times harder, and severely disabled people nineteen times harder. The impact of this on individuals, families and communities should be a major concern for Christians – something that informs what we choose to do in working for a more caring, more just society in line with the values of the Gospel. Here are some examples of how people have been affected, drawing on evidence from 2016 which continues to be reflected in data through to 2018.

People with disabilities or long-term illness

The benefit for people unable to work due to sickness or disability is now called Employment and Support Allowance (ESA). Everybody applying for this support must undergo a Work Capability Assessment (WCA), after which a Decision Maker in the Department for Work and Pensions (DWP) decides if a person is eligible to receive the benefit, or is fit to work. These assessments have now become notorious for producing inexplicable results, because the pressure to 'save money' is so great, because private contractors wish to maximise profit, and because successive governments have been determined to push as many people back into the jobs market as possible.

Linda Wootton was 49 and had undergone two heart and lung transplants when she was assessed. Despite suffering regular blackouts, renal failure and many other symptoms, she was declared 'fit to work' and her benefits were stopped.

Her husband Peter said: 'I sat there and listened to my wife drown in her own body fluids...The last months of her life were a misery because she worried about her benefits, feeling useless, like a scrounger. But there was no way in a million years she could work.'

There have been countless cases like Linda's, leaving people unable to work (according to the traditional definition of paid employment and its freelance equivalents) feeling intensely insecure and anxious. They fear they can be reassessed and declared 'fit for work' at any time, seemingly regardless of medical evidence to the contrary. They speak of their 'fear of the brown envelope', calling them in for an assessment that could take away their meagre income. Analysis has often shown that these assessments, performed by private companies, cost the taxpayer more than they save. They can also overlook or marginalise independent medical assessment, and they measure what sick and disabled people are able to contribute to society primarily in monetary terms. The whole process can be deeply dehumanising – far from the 'life in all its fullness' which the gospel message speaks about as God's desire.

Another big change affecting people who have an illness or disability is the abolition of Disability Living Allowance (DLA), which has been replaced by Personal Independence Payments (PIP). This benefit is designed to cover the considerable extra costs of living with a disability or illness, but the criteria for receiving PIP have been made much tighter. For example, a person with mobility difficulties, but who can walk 20 metres, no longer qualifies for higher rate mobility help. This means that at time of writing, between 400 and 500 adapted cars, powered wheelchairs and scooters were being taken away from people every week. People awaiting assessment are therefore intensely anxious, fearing that they could lose their independence and dignity.

Denise Hadden was born with bilateral femoral focal dysplasia, and is only 3 foot 8 inches tall. She cannot walk very far without severe pain, but has worked since she was sixteen. Losing her adapted car means she will have to give up her job as an Inclusion Manager at a Primary School, as she will no longer be able to get to work or travel to meetings.

These are the two main changes affecting disabled people, but there have been many others. The number of disabled people living in absolute poverty in the UK has risen sharply. Absolute poverty, as defined in official statistics, means having insufficient income to meet one's basic needs of food, clothing, and heating, etc.

Unemployed people and those in precarious employment

For people claiming Jobseeker's Allowance (JA), and for some disabled claimants, much tougher conditionality has been introduced. This means that if a person does not comply with everything asked of them by the Jobcentre they can have their benefit sanctioned (stopped) for between four weeks and three years. Sanctions have been applied in very large numbers, often for completely inappropriate reasons. Some documented reasons for sanctions include: missing a Jobcentre appointment because of being in hospital, attending a parent's funeral, attending a job interview, or accompanying a relative to hospital in a medical emergency. Not recording a Jobsearch on Christmas Day, or not looking for work whilst waiting for a new job to start, have also attracted a sanction.

Sanctions hit vulnerable people particularly hard, especially those with mental health problems or learning disabilities. In Wigan, a local Councillor reported: 'Several times this year I have had to refer a gentleman with learning difficulties to Denise (the local Christian minister) for food, due to him having sanctions on him for turning up late (once by four minutes).

'The gentleman can't tell the time and is a recluse. He has been found sitting in his flat in the dark with no electric or gas. He won't ask for help. The old neighbours watch out for him and contacted me - heaven knows what would have happened to him if they hadn't. I was informed he has to get a letter off the doctor for an electric card…The lad turned up at my door the other night. He hadn't eaten for five days. He looked like he was dying.'

The MP for the area said this was 'the fourth case of someone with learning

> *disabilities being sanctioned that I have come across in my constituency office this month.'*

Numerous studies have linked benefit sanctions to food bank use, crime, self-harm and suicide.

The growth of the so-called gig economy, zero hour contracts, virtually forced self-employment and seasonal working has also led to a considerable growth in precarious employment, and the emergence of the 'precariat'.

In-work poverty, child poverty

When talking about social security, it is easy to forget that working people on low incomes are also hit by cuts. In fact, a combination of low earnings and cuts to social security benefits now mean that almost two-thirds of children living in poverty are living in working households. The next few years are predicted to see the biggest rise in child poverty in a generation. Growing up in poverty can blight a child's educational and health prospects, leading to negative consequences, with costs for the individuals and society in general.

It is planned that over the next few years Universal Credit (UC) will replace several benefits, to make the system simpler. However, changes made to Universal Credit since it was originally designed mean that it will do very little if anything to reduce poverty. Universal Credit will replace Working Tax

Credits (WTC) for workers on a low income, and they too will become subject to sanctions.

Pensioners

Pensioners have been largely protected from cuts to the social security system as far as their incomes are concerned, but the most frail and vulnerable have suffered greatly from austerity. Very large cuts to social care budgets now mean that many frail people do not get the help they need to cope at home, putting them at risk of falls and increased trips to Accident and Emergency departments (A&E). When they go into hospital they are often unable to be discharged because the support they need is not there. They are then given the undignified label of 'bed blockers'.

So what can we do?

Across the UK, churches have responded to increasing poverty and hardship by setting up food banks, credit unions, job clubs, support centres and many other practical initiatives to help. These have been vital. It is disturbing to imagine what would have happened to people with no money and no food if they had not been able to visit a food bank.

But all these important initiatives deal mainly with the symptoms of the insecurity that is now a fact of life for the most disadvantaged people in society. With so many casual jobs and short-term or zero hours contracts, many workers, particularly younger people and those at the lower end of the income scale, find themselves frequently in and out of work. If the jobs market cannot deliver security for people, the social security system has to provide a reliable safety net to ensure that they are able to plan their futures and bring up families with some peace of mind.

In terms of the social security system as a whole, the economics of it, and what is being decided by government and public authorities, there are many reliable sources of information from three main sectors. First, there are official sources like the Office for National Statistics or the Institute for Fiscal Studies, although their material can make rather dry reading. For a more readable but equally accurate presentation of the facts, charities like Child Poverty Action Group provide excellent reports and comment on their website. Church bodies like the Joint Public Issues team, Church Action on Poverty and Ekklesia provide regular information and comment from a Christian perspective. Details are offered at the end of this course.

Having an accurate picture of what is happening will mean we can see what needs to change, and think about what kind of society we want. If we want security for our most vulnerable and disadvantaged neighbours (and for ourselves, if our lives take an unexpected turn) we need to express that wish and make it our priority, spiritually and practically, as we think about our God-given responsibility to our neighbours.

SESSION FOUR

Commenting

Starting with open discussion, response to both the biblical reading and commentary, and reactions to the reflection. Begin by asking people to identify points that particularly struck them as significant or important, and any flashes of inspiration or new insight ('light bulb moments').

Some issues for consideration:

- Apart from the practical help which so many churches and other charities (religious or otherwise) are offering, perhaps the most valuable thing we can do is become much better informed so that we can influence public debate and the policies of elected politicians and local/national authorities. What steps are needed to make this possible?

- Get to know more about what is happening to people. Try to talk to someone who has lost their adapted car, or has had their benefit sanctioned. For the bigger picture, do not rely on the press, politicians or mainstream media alone, but engage with civic organisations, advocacy organisations and self-activating groups like Spartacus Network (https://spartacusnetwork.wordpress.com/about/) and Disabled People Against Cuts https://dpac. uk.net).

- Unfortunately, this area is plagued with misleading information, which has coloured public understanding and influenced debate negatively. Newspapers frequently publish headline stories about 'welfare scroungers' and 'benefit fraudsters', only to print a very small retraction days or weeks later, after the original story has become accepted truth. Challenging newspaper reporting where it is misleading or scapegoating is important. The National Union of Journalists has a Code of Conduct (https://www.nuj.org.uk/about/nuj-code/) on fair and accurate reporting. Can you engage directly with reporters on these issues in a friendly but critical manner?

- 'Benefit cheating', which many tabloid newspapers regularly complain about, is shown by official figures to constitute a tiny percentage of the social security budget (under 1.5% according to the Office of National Statistics). By contrast, tax avoidance by the wealthy costs the country many billions of pounds every year. Yet proportionately far more is spent on tracking the former rather than the latter (https://tinyurl.com/lejgu2p). This tells us a lot about the prejudice that can distort our way of seeing. What should Christians be doing about this?

- A different approach is being taken to welfare in Scotland, albeit with its limited powers. This includes mitigating the Bedroom Tax, the refusal of sanctions, and a social security system being designed with the involvement of users (https://inews.co.uk/essentials/news/politics/scotland-bans-private-firms-benefit-assessments/). How can we learn and share best and better practice across these islands, and what role can churches play in this?

Challenging

- The Christian theologian Dietrich Bonhoeffer, writing out of the darkness of Germany in the 1930s, talked of the need to view life and history 'from the underside' – from the perspective of those pushed to the margins. This is where Jesus starts in the Gospel, too. It is surely where we as Christian people should begin, re-adjusting our vision in terms of real human need and the quest to right wrongs both individually and corporately?

- How can we start to tell another story, both about how life looks from the basement, and about a message of hope based on generosity and creativity rather than austerity and restraint?

Committing (Prayer)

Christ the cornerstone,
who gives strength and shape to our living,
may we who know the security and shelter of your
love
give succour and support to those
whom society disadvantages, displaces or
discards.
Amen.

WEEK FIVE

Cutting or Investing?

(Deciding how resources are used)

So if there is any encouragement in Christ, any comfort from love, any participation in the Spirit, any affection and sympathy, complete my joy by being of the same mind, having the same love, being in full accord and of one mind. Do nothing from selfish ambition or conceit, but in humility count others more significant than yourselves. Let each of you look not only to his own interests, but also to the interests of others.

Have this mind among yourselves, which is yours in Christ Jesus, who, though he was in the form of God, did not count equality with God a thing to be grasped, but emptied himself, by taking the form of a servant, being born in human likeness. And being found in human form, he humbled himself by becoming obedient to the point of death, even death on a cross. Therefore God has highly exalted him and bestowed on him the name that is above every name...
(Philippians 2:1-11)

This is how we know what love is: Jesus Christ laid down his life for us. And we ought to lay down our lives for our brothers and sisters. If anyone has material possessions and sees a brother or sister in need but has no pity on them, how can the love of God be in that person? Dear children, let us not love with words or speech but with actions and in truth.
(1 John 3:16-17)

Leader's Note

This session looks at cutting and investing, but has a particular emphasis on the scale, nature and impact of the cutbacks in public provision which have been carried out in recent years. It contrasts the filial nature of the community called together in the Body of Christ with the often-brutal reality of life felt by people with few resources and big problems. Session planning details are outlined in detail in the 'Course Guidance and Structure' chapter.

Gospel in Context

The biblical readings with which we began outline a series of Christian action, responses and virtues which open up a way of life where neighbourly responsibility, solidarity with those who are poor, vulnerable or badly paid, and concern for the good are all part of the DNA of a functioning community.

These characteristics are also linked directly to the person and work of Christ, his refusal of overbearing power, and his identification with the lowly in society. They suggest a location and orientation for the church which feels quite different to the religious power and status handed down through Christendom over the centuries.

This sense of identity and moral character for the Christian community is highly suggestive of the way we might respond to the issues about cutting or investing raised in the reflection on 'a national and local spending squeeze'.

The core issues of austerity as a mindset, an ideology and a policy framework are also explored in the opening chapter of this book, 'Moving Beyond Austerity: A Christian Challenge'. The cruelty of what is happening to those at the sharp end right now is disturbing. The reading from the first Epistle of John is particularly powerful in orienting us towards where our sympathy and action might lie.

Reflection:
A national and local spending squeeze – *Virginia Moffatt*

From the famous parable of the Good Samaritan, right through to the appeal in chapter 25 of Matthew's Gospel that we looked at in the last session, Jesus' message could not be clearer. His followers have a primary responsibility to look after each other, yes – but also to show God's practical care for strangers, aliens and even enemies. Indeed it is our response to those who we do not have an immediate or familial interest in which may be the true litmus test of love-in-action, the fruits of a faith shaped by the living Christ.

Early Christians chose to show what love of neighbour meant in practice by living communally. 'All those who had believed were together, and had all things in common, and they began selling their property and possessions, and were sharing them with all, as anyone might have need,' we read in Acts chapter two. Today Christians in our part of the world live in complex, multi-layered societies that militate against holding things in common. Yet we are still called to care for our brothers and sisters in need – in a culture where the scale of that need is more visible than ever before. How, then, should we respond?

The first challenge is to do what can be done within our local communities. However, that too will be difficult. We have families, jobs and commitments that demand a lot of attention. There is only so much that we can achieve individually. Which is why we need to recognise that if we are to build a society where each person has access to adequate housing, education, food, healthcare, social support, cultural enrichment and meaningful activity, then we need collective responses to make that possible.

Perhaps we could see the social and economic solidarity needed to love our neighbours (both strangers and friends) as a modern way of 'holding goods in common'? If so, we need corporate means of enabling wealth to be pooled, shared and distributed throughout society. This was the realisation that motivated people like Archbishop William Temple (mentioned earlier in this book) to develop the thinking behind what came to be known as 'the welfare state' – governance and provision by and for good neighbours.

The true vision here was of a welfare society, a public path to enabling all to fare well in personal, social and spiritual terms; not simply a 'safety net' for those who fell behind. Christian belief, belonging and behaviour was seen as a key motivator and guarantor of such a vision.

There are many questions that can be asked about the nature of this vision, its Christian grounding in a mixed belief society, and how public welfare can be sought and secured in a corporately driven, consumer-based economy. But let's start, as the early Christians did, with the local.

Every few years people across Britain elect local, regional, devolved and national authorities to work on our behalf, using (among other resources) money they collect from the taxes we pay. We last had such elections in May 2017. The amount of money available to spend on public services is both a political choice and a function of the way we create, distribute and use money. In the UK, public spending has fluctuated between 36.6 per cent and 49.9 per cent of national income since the Second World War, according to the Institute for Fiscal Studies (IFS).

In these elections some parties press for a larger spend on public services, arguing that we have a collective responsibility for meeting society's needs, which could in theory affect any of us at any time. Others press for spending less, believing that too much state intervention limits individual freedom and enterprise, encouraging dependency.

In times of plenty, decisions about public spending are easier, as the government has room to manoeuvre, but in times of economic hardship these decisions become starker. Does a fragile economy need investment or cutting in order to produce growth? Those who call for investment point out that if money is spent on public services, there will be more people in work, they will put money back into the economy, and a /multiplier' effect begins to kick in. Growth in one area stimulates growth in other areas. This in turn means there will be fewer people claiming benefits, which reduces the welfare bill. More people will also able to buy goods, which benefits others and provides more taxes to collect which reduces the deficit. The counter argument is that the best way to support the economy is to reduce public sector expenditure, which will reduce the deficit. Any jobs lost will be replaced by more efficient private sector roles. This will help growth, which will also be aided by tax cuts for businesses and higher earners.

Assessing the Impact

So what's the evidence? Well, the Coalition Government that was in power from 2010 to 2015, and the Conservative Government that followed, both broadly chose the second approach. As a result we have seen a steady decline in public services funding from 48.1 per cent in 2010/11 to 40.4 per cent in 2016. (IFS, 2015) Local government has been one of the biggest losers, with funding reduced by 27 per cent in this period, a change that has affected adult and children's social care, public transport, services to the homeless, home care, cultural services, libraries, recreation and sports, parks, waste collections, planning and parking. (Hastings et al, 2015)

There cannot be a single community that hasn't felt the impact of these cuts. For example, the BBC reported in early 2016 that 343 libraries have closed since 2010, with the loss of 8,000 jobs and a further 111 planned in the same year. That trend has continued into 2017. Libraries play a vital part in communities, as the author Jeanette Winterson has argued, noting they provide a cultural space,

> 'For kids with nowhere to go, kids who don't have books or a room of their own, for stressed-out parents, for students needing a place to study and find more than Google can offer, for older people who want a safe place outside of the house' (Winterson, 2012)

Although we are all seeing our local services diminished, and councils put under huge pressure, it is the poorest who have suffered most from the cuts. The most deprived areas have lost the greatest amount of funding, and poor people have been disproportionately affected by cuts social care services. (Hastings et al, 2015). Although David Cameron promised 'we are all in this together' it is in fact sick and disabled people, who have borne the largest burden (Duffy, 2014).

Between 2011 and 2015 £3.5 billion has been taken from social care services that were already under pressure. As a result of these cuts, which are set to continue and deepen in 2017/18, a study by a consortium of disability charities found that 40 per cent of disabled adults are unable to wash, dress or leave the house due to lack of carers (Brawn et al, 2013). The experience of Kenneth, a young man with cerebral palsy is typical. When he left his family home to live in a shared house with support he often found his housemates left with their wheelchairs facing the wall. Since moving to a new service, the best he says he can hope for, is to choose what time he gets up in the morning and what to have for lunch (Ryan, 2015).

By 2016, the situation had reached such a critical point that David Cameron even faced criticism from his own local council. Not only that, but his mother signed a petition against the closure of children's centres and his aunt joined protests about the same subject. So this is a concern that crosses party lines (Slawson, 2016).

The previous government came into office pledging to care for the poor and most vulnerable in society. The day after David Cameron stepped down, and before Theresa May took office, the *Guardian* newspaper published the story of Luke, a disabled man living in Oxfordshire. As a result of cuts, Luke is unable to receive care to get out of the house, eat, drink or even go to the toilet (Ryan, 2016). The fact he was advised by social workers that he could urinate in a tea urn, provides a shocking example of how badly austerity policies have failed society at the human level.

The trend has continued in 2017. As we noted in passing earlier, five areas in the middle of England are planning to cut spending on mental health services in 2017/18, despite being told by NHS England to ensure that they increase spending in line with physical health spending, and despite a significant increase in media and public concern about mental health issues and their severe impact on growing sections of the population.

Meanwhile, the crisis in local government is deep and abiding. Some councils may need to declare themselves technically bankrupt. A survey of councils in England and Wales by the Local Government Information Unit (LGIU) think-tank found that three-quarters had little or no confidence in the sustainability of local government finances and more than one in 10 believed they were in danger of failing to meet legal requirements to deliver core services (Butler, 2017). In Scotland the situation is slightly less dire, with larger cash reserves, but still very tight indeed, with continuing economies.

We have been told since 2010 that cuts were necessary to reduce the deficit. And yet in early 2016 the deficit was higher than before the crash in 2008, with many economists believing that all projections are off the table post-Brexit. In any case, as Simon Barrow argues in the introductory chapter, cutting the deficit rarely helps cut overall debt because it starves the economy of resources, investment and spending, hampering the expansion that is needed to pay down debt. So it is not surprising that, contrary to what many suppose, the national debt continues to rise (UK Public Spending website 2016). It now stands at £1.8 trillion, almost double the figure inherited six years earlier.

Austerity is not only cruel to those who can least afford to face cuts. It is also a failed policy on its own terms, as Nobel Prize winning economists such as Joseph Stiglitz and Paul Krugman have long documented, and as bodies such as Ekklesia's friends at the New Economics Foundation (NEF, 2016) and PRIME Economics are saying. It is therefore surely time, from an ethically renewed economic perspective, to call on all parties for an end to austerity and a commitment to reinvest sensibly in local government, public services and green-edged technology.

References

'Public Spending Under Labour', Election Briefing Note No. 5 (BN92), by Robert Chote,

Rowena Crawford, Carl Emmerson, Gemma Tetlow (Institute for Fiscal Studies, 2010).

'This government has delivered substantial spending cuts; big differences in parties' plans for next parliament '(Institute for Fiscal Studies, 15 September 2015).

'The cost of the cuts: the impact on local government and poorer communities', by Annette Hastings, Nick Bailey, Glen Bramley, Maria Gannon and David Watkins (Joseph Rowntree Foundation, 23 March 2015).

'We must protect and reinvent our local libraries', by Jeanette Winterson (The *Guardian*, 23 November 2012).

'Counting the Cuts', by Simon Duffy (Centre for Welfare Reform 2014 – and 2017/18 updated analysis at: http://www.centreforwelfarereform.org/library).

'The other care crisis: Making social care funding work for disabled adults in England', by Ellie Brawn, Marc Bush, Caroline Hawkings and Robert Trotter (Scope, Mencap, National Autistic Society, Sense, Leonard Cheshire, 2013).

'The Disability Audit: the eight coalition policies that have hit disabled people', by Frances Ryan (*New Statesman*, 29 April 2015) and 'Cuts Target Disabled People', by Simon Duffy (Centre for Welfare Reform, 2017, http://www.centreforwelfarereform.org/library/by-az/film-cuts-target-disabled-people.html).

'Life in David Cameron's back yard is set to get tougher – who will feel the pain?' by Nicola Slawson (The *Guardian*, 10 February 2016).

'Councils 'at breaking point' due to budget cuts and rising social care bills', by Patrick Butler (The *Guardian*, 10 February 2017).

Recent UK Budget Deficits: UK Public Spending (ukpublicspending.org.uk)

'Luke can't move, drink or use the loo. The council offered him a tea urn', by Frances Ryan (The *Guardian*, 14 July 2016).

'Public Spending for Public Benefit' (New Economics Foundation, 2016).

'CCGs cutting spending on mental health despite NHS pledges', by Carolyn Wickware (*Pulse*, 27 April 2017).

SESSION FIVE

Commenting

Our final opportunity for open discussion, inviting people to respond both to the biblical reading and commentary, and to the reflection. Begin by asking people to identify points that particularly struck them as significant or important, and any flashes of inspiration or new insight ('light bulb moments').

Some concerns for consideration:

- The Institute for Fiscal Studies (which tries hard to be non-partisan) has highlighted the disproportionate impact of local government and other public spending cuts on the most vulnerable. How can our churches act more effectively to speak up alongside disabled people and others feeling the brunt of retrenchment?

- In what way is the welfare state the outcome of a Christian vision of how we should live together?

- 'Welfare' and 'social security' are often seen as negative or stigmatising words these days. How can we recover a sense that they matter for *all* of us, and are not just about a safety net as a last resort?

- In what ways is it practical for Christians and others to think about sharing and holding goods in common, in the way the Early Church did in its initial phase? How can we encourage more mutuality within and beyond the Christian community?

Challenging

Responding to the issues raised in this chapter feels like a huge task. So what can we Christians do? Here are a few ideas:

- Join an advocacy group about an issue you are concerned for (a number are listed in the resource section at the end of this book).

- Find out what cuts have happened in your local community and who has been most affected by them, write to your local Council asking them to discuss with you and others how to protect services, and to your local MP asking them to seek more investment in local authority funding.

- Write to the Prime Minister and other senior figures about the issues in your area, and about concerns you have coming out of this course.

- Organise prayer services, displays and speakers at your church, to educate your community about the issues and to get them involved.

- Volunteer in projects set up to help the victims of austerity.

- Review the challenges in other parts of this course for possible actions or responses you may have missed.

WEEK FIVE

Committing (Prayer)

Jesus of Jerusalem and Gethsemane,
who consciously chose the way of the cross:
May we never forget that the world we inhabit
is not the product of blind fate
but shaped by the choices we make;
And, like you, may we also choose that which
        advances God's Kingdom
Even when it seems neither sensible nor safe.
Amen.

AFTERWORD

Beyond the Good Samaritan: the caring economy

JOHN GILLIBRAND

I am the father of Adam, who is a young man – he has just reached his 24th year – on the autistic spectrum. He has also has substantial learning disabilities and highly challenging behaviours, combined with an almost complete absence of a sense of danger. A year ago his vocabulary expanded slightly from 40 to 50 words. Even in austerity Britain, we can be confident that the package of support which he receives, in full time residential care, will continue, because without it his safety could not be guaranteed.

Yet Adam stands for the thousands of people in these islands the quality of whose life depends on the quality of the public services which he receives. There is a famous story, at the end of the last Labour government, and two years after the 2008 crash, of the then Chief Secretary to the Treasury, Liam Bryne, leaving a note for his successor with the simple message: 'I am afraid there is no money.' (It's actually an old transition, but it still runs close to the bone.)

The sharp question is this. How do we as Christians respond when we are told that economic conditions do not permit the provision of essential services to those in need?

To seek an answer for that, I am going to turn to the story of the Good Samaritan in Luke Chapter Ten – possibly the most famous one in the New Testament, and with a significant resonance well beyond Christian circles. It is set in the context of a discussion between Jesus and a lawyer. Seeking to test Jesus, the lawyer asks: 'Teacher, what shall I do to inherit eternal life?' Although it is a trick question, the answer which Jesus gives to such a question will take us to the core of his beliefs and message:

> *[Jesus] said to him, 'What is written in the law? How do you read?' And [the lawyer] answered, 'You shall love the Lord your God with all your heart, and with all your soul, and with all your strength, and with all your mind; and your neighbour as yourself.' And he said to him, 'You have answered right; do this, and you will live.*

Our starting point, therefore, is our collective solidarity in relationship to God and to each other. On such a view of the world, if a disabled person is losing access to a much needed day service following local authority cuts, that matters to us all, and we are not allowed to treat the provision of services to that person as a problem, for love does not allow us to treat any other person as a problem.

In the story which Jesus then tells, the man stripped of his clothes and left half dead by robbers on the road from Jerusalem to Jericho does not receive help from the expected sources – the priest and Levite walk by, on the other side. It is the Samaritan who goes to him, and by so doing is able to assess the real extent of his need. We see care as a universal human need functioning across cultural boundaries. To this way of thinking, a migrant is not putting pressure on local services – schools, hospitals, social services – but has needs to be met come what may.

The Good Samaritan provides some of the care himself, without reimbursement. 'He saw him, he had compassion, and went to him and bound up his wounds, pouring on oil and wine; then he set him on his own beast and brought him to an inn, and took care of him.'

According to the 2011 Census, there were 6,506,257 carers in the UK, with the care provided being worth an estimated £119 billion a year. 1.4 million people among this total provide over 50 hours of care a week. The Good Samaritan did not plan to provide care: in the circumstances in which he found himself, it was what love called him to do. It is in the nature of that love not to stint – there have been no austerity cutbacks in the work of unpaid carers in the UK.

However, for whatever reason, the Good Samaritan cannot do it all himself. He has to be elsewhere. At that point he makes provision for paid care to take place: 'The next day he took out two denarii and gave them to the innkeeper.' Margaret Thatcher once notoriously said that 'nobody would remember the Good Samaritan if he had only good intentions. He had money as well.' She perhaps missed the point, because of the extraordinary words with which the Good Samaritan follows up his kind offer: 'Look after him, (…) and when I return, I will reimburse you for any extra expense you may have.' The story which Jesus tells is a story of care offered without a budget being set, where there are no notes left behind saying that there is no money left. The limit of care is not the cash limit, but only the limit set by global human and physical resources when we remain in solidarity with each other, and – like the Good Samaritan – have the compassion to identify and respond to the need.

This was a story, and became one of the most famous stories ever told. But at the end of his story, Jesus makes this challenge to the lawyer: 'Go, and do likewise.' After the ethical reflection on God's Word, after the sharing of a story, we are in turn challenged to go and do something about it. To change discussion and story telling – of which there is no shortage – into deeds.

Yet how can we do that? Margaret Thatcher reading these words would say that you can't do anything about the reality of the economic system, that you have to live within your financial means, that we can do nothing about the iron laws of the market. A Christian who hears the word 'law' should always hear at the same time the word 'grace'. Maybe we are being called by the circumstances of austerity Britain to a different kind of economics which starts not with limited financial resources but with the abundance of human need, in a world of resources abundant if only shared. We start with the people beaten up and left half dead at the side of the road, and build our economic thinking around them.

Current economic thinking throughout the system is so much built around desire. From the 1980's onwards, market economics thought of individuals in competition with each other, with each individual seeking sufficient prosperity to fulfil her/his desires. Ironically, the biggest and most controversial issue which the churches have faced in the same period, in all the debates about human sexuality, is the question of desire. We need to build our economics around needs, rather than desires. We need to build our church life in a solidarity with one another in our commitment to the meeting of human need. A new economics and a new ecclesiology go hand in hand.

AFTERWORD

And such an economics is practicable, is realistic. Since 2008, we have succeeded – more or less – in stabilising the economy, rather than addressing the systemic flaws which gave rise to the crisis in the first place. That is, so to speak, austerity's achievement, but that is all that has been achieved, and it is looking highly precarious. The Office for Budget Responsibility's Forecast from back in March 2016 commented that 'the period of weak productivity growth post-crisis [is] continuing to lengthen.' There is a corresponding gloomy prospect for Gross Domestic Product. The OBR have been prompted 'to revise down our GDP growth forecasts by around 0.3 percentage points a year to an average of 2.1 per cent a year over the rest of the decade.' Subsequent forecasts in 2017 have wavered. PRIME Economics expect growth to slow by at least 0.5 per cent in 2018. Government spending growth will be stronger than in 2016, and (with the exception of 2014 ahead of the election) will be second strongest since austerity began. But with deflation in the world economy, the coming Brexit hit, the London-centred housing construction bubble flagging, and business investment fragile, the boost from the fall in the value of the pound after the EU referendum is being offset by low global and UK demand. It's not a pretty picture.

We are in a situation in which it may well be necessary to inject positive demand into the economy. The economy is in of need a motor. In the Industrial Revolution it was provided by the heavy extraction and manufacturing industries; as they declined, it was provided – until the crash of 2008 – by the financial sector, in the case of the United Kingdom, by the City of London. Might it be that the new motor (in addition to much needed green investment) will be the provision of care? The demand is certainly there and increasing. Once we start assessing need in order to meet it by the provision of a well-waged and well-trained care workforce, we can provide the economy with the stimulus that is so sorely needs, by injecting care into our communities rather than cash into our financial institutions. This is not dreamy idealism: it may well be that there is no alternative.

People with disabilities often despair of the culture of benevolence, which treats them as a problem, which turns them into an object of pity and charity. In the model of the Good Samaritan story, there is no place for objectification: we are called to love our neighbour *as we love ourselves*. This is not just a call to individual holiness and loving kindness to others. It is the thought of a society and an economy bound together by ties of loving solidarity. In this context, people with disabilities are no longer the problem, but mutual support becomes the solution to society's problem.

Over many years, the Christian Churches have grappled with numerical decline, and with an associated decline of influence in wider society. The debates over sexuality have not helped. Many younger people are incredulous that the church is seriously debating issues that for them have long been closed matters, not susceptible of debate, as well as propounding views that are – objectively considered – not distinctively Christian. For the sake of its mission, the Church needs to discover its unique voice, its special contribution to public debate. God is love. In working for a society and economy built around caring for one another, we make that love an incarnate reality – we proclaim Christ, and see God's love reflected in every moment that care is given and received. Austerity offers no future. It is time to say some new words.

ADDITIONAL PRAYERS

Affirmation

The collects at the end of each of the sessions in this course, plus the material here, have been specially prepared by Pat Bennett, with slight adjustments. Some readers will wish to use these prayers in an extended Liturgy to accompany one or more sessions, or for a Sunday or midweek service. We are also happy to commend Pat's worship materials published by Wild Goose Publications on behalf of the Iona Community. https://tinyurl.com/patbennettWGP

THE ECONOMY OF GOD

As citizens of God's Commonwealth

We are called not to legitimate austerity
but to liberate life;

not to serve the system
but to succour the weak;

not to privilege ourselves
but to prioritise need;

not to worship wealth

but to 'waste' perfume;
not to grasp our possessions
but to give away our lives.

As citizens of the Commonwealth of God
We are not ruled by the economies of the world,
but released by the Economy of the Word
that is spoken in and as Jesus.

CONFESSION

God the listener,
whose heart is tuned to the cries of the poor,
we confess that sometimes
we have stopped our ears
to voices from beyond the margins….

Kyrie eleison, Christe eleison
(Lord have mercy, Christ have mercy)

Silence

God the observer,
who gathers and stores the tears of the distressed,
we confess that sometimes
we have averted our eyes
from injustices on our own doorsteps…

Silence or a Kyrie

God the giver,
whose generosity accepts no constraint,
we confess that sometimes
we have kept our hands closed

towards those who have less than enough…
Silence or a Kyrie
God the welcomer,
who keeps an open door,
we confess that sometimes
we have walled off our hearts
from the urgings of hospitality

Silence or a Kyrie

God the disturber,
who values justice and mercy above sacrifice and
singing,
we confess that sometimes
we have kept our minds armoured
against the imperatives demanded by your
Kingdom

Silence or a Kyrie

God the restorer,
who takes what is broken and remakes and
repurposes it,
forgive us where we have fallen short
renew our sense of what is right
and give us the courage to act
as you would have us do.

Amen

FURTHER RESOURCES

Books

Mark Blyth, *Austerity: The History of a Dangerous Idea* (Oxford University Press, 2015)

Andrew Francis, *Foxes Have Holes: Christian Reflections on Britain's Housing Need* (Ekklesia, 2016)

Peter Herriot, *All in This Together* (Darton, Longman and Todd, 2016)

Kerry-Anne Mendoza, *Austerity: The Demotion of Welfare and the Rise of the Zombie Economy* (New Internationalist, 2015)

Virginia Moffatt (ed.), *Reclaiming the Common Good: How Christians Can Re-Build Our Broken World* (Darton, Longman and Todd, 2017)

Richard Murphy, *The Courageous State: Rethinking Economics, Society and the Role of Government* (Searching Finance Ltd, 2011)

Richard Murphy, *The Joy of Tax* (Bantam Press, 2015)

Ched Myers, *Sabbath Economics* (Bartimeus Collective, 2011)

Mary O'Hara, *Austerity Bites: A Journey to the Sharp End of Cuts in the UK* (Policy Press, 2015)

Ann Pettifor, *Just Money: How Society Can Break the Despotic Power of Finance* (Commonwealth Books, 2014)

Ann Pettifor, *The Production of Money: How to Break the Power of Bankers* (Verso, 2017)

Florian Schui, *Austerity: The Great Failure* (Yale University Press, 2015)

Peter Selby, *Grace and Mortgage* (Darton, Longman and Todd, 2009)

FURTHER RESOURCES

Yanis Varoufakis, *And the Weak Suffer What They Must?: Europe, Austerity and the Threat to Global Stability* (Vintage, 2017)

Organisations and websites

Bartimaeus Cooperative Ministries: http://www.bcm-net.org

Centre for Welfare Reform: http://www.centreforwelfarereform.org

Church Action on Poverty: http://www.church-poverty.org.uk

Christian Aid: https://www.christianaid.org.uk

Copolla Comment: http://www.coppolacomment.com

Disabled People Against Cuts: https://dpac.uk.net

Ekklesia: http://www.ekklesia.co.uk

End Hunger UK: http://endhungeruk.org

FareShare: http://www.fareshare.org.uk

Green New Deal Group: http://www.greennewdealgroup.org

Joint Public Issues Team: http://www.jointpublicissues.org.uk

Joseph Rowntree Foundation: https://www.jrf.org.uk/

Iona Community: https://iona.org.uk

New Economics Foundation: http://neweconomics.org

Ann Pettifor – Debtonation: http://www.debtonation.org

Poverty Truth Commission: http://www.faithincommunityscotland.org/poverty-truth-commission/

PRIME Economics: http://www.primeeconomics.org

Spartacus Network: https://spartacusnetwork.wordpress.com/about/)

Tax Justice Network: http://www.taxjustice.net

Tax Research UK: http://www.taxresearch.org.uk/

ToUChstone: http://touchstoneblog.org.uk

Trussell Trust: https://www.trusselltrust.org

UK Public Spending: http//ukpublicspending.org.uk

(A more detailed resource list is available via www.ekklesia.co.uk/lent2018)

CONTRIBUTORS

Simon Barrow is Director of Ekklesia. A widely published writer, journalist and commentator on public issues, he was formerly assistant general secretary of Churches Together in Britain and Ireland. His books include *A Nation Changed?* (with Gerry Hassan, 2017), *Scotland 2021* (with Mike Small, 2016), *Fear or Freedom?* (2009) and *Consuming Passion* (with Jonathan Bartley, DLT 2005).

Pat Bennett is Programme Development Worker for the Iona Community, based in Glasgow. She has published extensively in the area of liturgy and worship, and is creator of *Transformed by Life: An Easter Communion liturgy* (Wild Goose Publications 2016), among many others.

John Gillibrand is an Anglican priest with the Church in Wales. An Ekklesia associate and academic, his book *Disabled Church – Disabled Society: The Implications of Autism for Philosophy, Theology and Politics*, with a foreword by Rowan Williams, was nominated in 2013 for the Michael Ramsey Prize.

Savitri Hensman is a widely published Christian commentator on politics, religion, welfare and allied topics. An Ekklesia associate, she works in the care and equalities sector. She is author of *Sexuality, Struggle and Saintliness* (2016).

Keith Hebden is an Anglican priest, author and activist, and is the Director of the Urban Theology Union in Sheffield. He is an Ekklesia associate and co-founded End Hunger Fast. His books include *Re-enchanting the Activist: Spirituality and Social Change* (2016) and *Seeking Justice: The Radical Compassion of Jesus* (2013).

Bernadette Meaden has written about political, religious and social issues for some years, and is strongly influenced by Christian Socialism, liberation theology and the Catholic Worker movement. She is an Ekklesia associate and regular contributor.

Virginia Moffatt is an active advocate for peace, justice and inclusive welfare. She is an author, Ekklesia associate, and has worked in social care for many years. Her books include *Echo Hall* (2018), *Reclaiming the Common Good* (DLT 2017) and *Rapture and What Comes After* (2014).

Jill Segger is an Associate Director of Ekklesia with particular involvement in editorial issues. She is a freelance writer who contributes to *The Church Times*, *The Catholic Herald*, *Reform* and *The Friend*, among other publications. Jill is an active Quaker.

ABOUT EKKLESIA

Based in Edinburgh and London, Ekklesia is an independent, not-for-profit Christian think-tank promoting transformative ideas in politics, society, economy and religion.

We advocate a church on the side of those at the margins, and solutions to societal challenges based on a strong commitment to social justice, inclusion, nonviolence, environmental action, participatory democracy and a creative exchange among those of different convictions (religious and otherwise).

Ekklesia is committed to promoting new models of mutual economy, conflict transformation, peacemaking, social power, restorative justice, community engagement, and truth-telling in politics.

We are also working to encourage alternative perspectives on humanitarian challenges in a globalised world, not least a positive, affirming approach to migration.

Overall, we are concerned with the policy, practice and philosophy of moving beyond 'top-down' politics, economics and systems of belief.

This means that, while we are a public issues think-tank rooted in an Anabaptist-influenced Christian outlook, we are keen to work with people of many backgrounds who share common principles and approaches.

Ekklesia's reports, analysis and commentary can be accessed via our website here: www.ekklesia.co.uk

starting to turn. New and complex identities are being developed and, as cuts to services start to affect almost everyone, different institutions such as the Church, advocacy organisations and academia are collaborating to challenge the dominant narrative.

Fully up-to-date to include fresh reflections on both continued austerity, Brexit and the ensuing economic, social, religious and political turmoil as well as projections for a post-Brexit future, *All In This Together?* sets out to challenge the need for, and indeed continued relevance of, the Government's austerity administration – a political elite that has presided over what Herriot terms the 'Second Age of Austerity' since 2010.

'Peter Herriot demonstrates the dangers of dividing a country against itself and the dilemmas facing church leaders and others who are trying to halt our slide into deeper levels of social injustice.'
Dr Simon Duffy, Director of the Centre for Welfare Reform.

'This book powerfully exposes the disturbing realities of a deeply divided Britain in an age of austerity. However it is not despairing, holding out the hope of building a sense of identity based on valuing everyone equally.'
Savi Hensman, writer, activist, voluntary sector worker, and Ekklesia associate.

Peter Herriot rightly points out that it is only when we bring civil society together, through allied institutions speaking confidently against injustice that we can bring an alternative. I recommend this book to any leader in civil society keen to take a stand.'
Rev Dr Keith Hebden, Director of Urban Theology Unit, Sheffield, and author of Seeking Justice: The Radical Compassion of Jesus.

ALL IN THIS TOGETHER?

Author: Peter Herriot
Publisher: Darton, Longman and Todd Ltd
Published: July 2016
144 pages
ISBN: 978-0-232-53259-3

Today we are in what some have described as 'the second age of austerity' in Britain. The collapse of traditional identities, and the creation by those in power of new labels such as 'skivers', 'shirkers' and 'hard-working families' has created a divisive narrative with devastating personal impact, giving the lie to the political campaign slogan: 'We're all in this together'. Moreover, the conduct and outcome of the EU referendum in 2016 is likely to ensure divisive effects of inequality and austerity are further reinforced and enlarged.

However, Peter Herriot believes the tide is